PRAISE FOR
MINDFULLY SUCCESSFUL

"This book is the ultimate toolbox for tapping into the power of your brain, body, and breath to go from successfully exhausted to mindfully successful."

MEL ROBBINS, New York Times bestselling
author and host of *The Mel Robbins Podcast*

"Margo offers a unique approach to leadership that seamlessly blends scientific research with practical, actionable strategies. *Mindfully Successful* empowers leaders to implement evidence-based principles in their everyday lives, allowing them to lead with both mind and heart and finding the best approach in both."

DR. MARSHALL GOLDSMITH, Thinkers50 #1 executive
coach and New York Times bestselling author of *The Earned
Life, Triggers,* and *What Got You Here Won't Get You There*

"As a leadership book, *Mindfully Successful* stands out by translating scientific principles and offering practical ways to harness your natural resources—brain, body, and breath—to be more successful without exhausting yourself or those you lead."

CY WAKEMAN, CEO, Reality-Based
Leadership, and author of *No Ego*

"Success without well-being is not success. *Mindfully Successful* is filled with practical, science-based strategies and exercises to navigate the pursuit of achievement while radiating the mix of balance, strength, and confidence that is the key to great and lasting leadership."

SHAWN ACHOR, New York Times bestselling author
of *Big Potential* and *The Happiness Advantage*

"Margo Boster has crafted a transformative blueprint for leaders who seek to navigate the high demands of their roles with grace, resilience, and mindfulness. By integrating the science of the mind, body, and breath, *Mindfully Successful* provides the tools needed to enhance mental clarity, physical well-being, and authentic leadership. This book is a beacon for anyone committed to realizing their full potential and making a meaningful impact!"

MAJ. GEN. (RET) APRIL VOGEL, Air National Guard

"In *Mindfully Successful*, Margo Boster offers a highly accessible and practical 'user's manual' for integrating your mind, body, and breath to support the outcomes you're hoping to achieve for yourself and your team. A must-read for leaders."

SCOTT EBLIN, executive coach and bestselling author of
The Next Level and *Overworked and Overwhelmed*

"*Mindfully Successful* is recommended reading if you want to become a wiser leader, coworker, friend, or person! I've greatly enjoyed Margo's holistic wisdom in her guest articles for our blog on organizational development, leadership, and change. She doesn't use hollow phrases but instead combines science with practical application. Don't just read this book—reflect on it and do the exercises!"

MARCELLA BREMER, MScBA, cofounder, OCAI online; culture and change consultant; and author of *Organizational Culture Change*

"I've seen firsthand, over many years, the transformative impact of Margo Boster's coaching and mentoring. *Mindfully Successful* synthesizes her accumulated expertise into an essential guide for leaders who seek to balance their professional demands with personal well-being. Margo's deep understanding of the connections between neuroscience, mindfulness, and leadership provides an invaluable intersection of useful insight throughout the book. These complex topics are described in practical terms so that leaders can formulate strategies to conquer self-doubt, reduce stress, and enhance their personal and professional achievements. This book gets my highest and most enthusiastic recommendation."

J.R. FLATTER, founder and CEO, Flatter Leadership Academy

"In *Mindfully Successful*, Margo Boster provides a refreshing and vital perspective on leadership. This book adeptly combines the latest findings in neuroscience with the ancient practices of mindfulness and yoga, offering a powerful toolkit for leaders seeking to break free from the cycle of stress and burnout. Margo's approach is not only practical and evidence-based but also deeply compassionate. Her extensive experience and innovative techniques make this book a transformative resource for leaders at any stage of their journey."

LEAH GERBER, PhD, professor of conservation science and founding director of the Center for Biodiversity Outcomes, Arizona State University

www.amplifypublishinggroup.com

Mindfully Successful: Unlock the Power of Your Brain, Body, and Breath to Elevate Your Leadership

©2025 Margo Boster. All Rights Reserved. No part of this publication may be reproduced, stored in a retrieval system or transmitted in any form by any means electronic, mechanical, or photocopying, recording or otherwise without the permission of the author.

This book is not intended as a substitute for the medical advice of physicians. The reader should regularly consult a physician in matters relating to their health and particularly with respect to any symptoms that may require diagnosis or medical attention. The author and publisher advise readers to take full responsibility for their safety and know their limits. Do not take risks beyond your level of experience, aptitude, training, and comfort level.

For more information, please contact:
Amplify Publishing, an imprint of Amplify Publishing Group
620 Herndon Parkway, Suite 220
Herndon, VA 20170
info@amplifypublishing.com

Library of Congress Control Number: 2024913664

CPSIA Code: PRV0824A

ISBN-13: 979-8-89138-367-8

Printed in the United States

To my husband, Mark, who gave me the gift of love,
taught me the power of love,
and always saw brilliance in me even when I didn't.

To my son, Danny, and my daughter, Nicole,
for never letting me lose sight of my goal.

And for my grandson, Elliott, because science never lies.

MINDFULLY SUCCESSFUL

Unlock the Power of Your
BRAIN, BODY, and **BREATH**
to Elevate Your Leadership

MARGO BOSTER

CONTENTS

Introduction xi

1. Mindfully Successful 1
A Road Map 9
Brain, Body, and Breath 13
The Integrator 15

2. Brain 19
A Closer Look at the Brain 24
Our Three Brains 26
Working Together 30
Distinction between the Brain, Mind, and Thoughts 33
Learned Behaviors—Ingraining the Pathways 36
The Power of Neuroplasticity 40
Quick to Judge 44
    Perception → Recognition → Action 46
    Noticing or Judging? 48
Training the Brain 50
    Technique One: Noticing 50
    Technique Two: Naming 53
    Technique Three: Scratch the Record 57
    Technique Four: Meditation 61
Summary 69

3. Body **71**

Your Nervous Systems 76

The Autonomic Nervous System (ANS) 80

Sympathetic Nervous System 83

Parasympathetic Nervous System 85

Physical Awareness 86

Physical Movement 89

What to Do 90

There's a Pose for That 91

To Feel Centered 94

To Feel Strong or Confident 97

Energized and Powerful Voice 98

Humility or Patience 100

Release of Emotions or Cooling 101

Cleansing (Emotional or Physical) 104

To Feel Balanced 105

Releasing / Letting Go 106

Is Yoga the Only Answer? 106

Summary 107

4. Breath ... **109**

"Take a Breath" ... 111

The Three Diaphragms ... 116

Breathing Practices ... 123

To Feel Calmed and Reduce Anxiety—
4-4-7 Breathing ... 124

To Return Breathing to Normal after
Stressful Experience—Box Breathing ... 126

To Feel Energized and Relieve Anger—
Lion's Breath (Simhasana) ... 127

To Feel Balanced and Activate Both
Sides of Your Brain—Alternate Nostril
Breathing (Nadi Shodhana) ... 128

*To Feel Calm **or** to Feel Energized*
(Viloma Breathing) ... 130

Summary ... 132

5. The Integration ... **135**

Mindfully Successful Chris ... 136

Successfully Exhausted Chris ... 139

Mindfully Successful Chris—Continued ... 140

Summary ... 143

Acknowledgments ... 145

About the Author ... 149

INTRODUCTION

My explorations of the science of brain, body, and breath began in earnest in what is typically considered a more metaphysical practice. Following a life-altering car accident when I was thirty years old, I began practicing yoga to reclaim my physical and mental health. Over nearly a decade, I immersed myself in exploring its poses (*asanas*), breathwork (*pranayama*), meditation (*dharana/dhyana*), and philosophy (the Eight Limbs). Seeking a deeper understanding, I completed a yearlong yoga teacher training program in 2010. About the time the yoga teacher training was wrapping up, I enrolled in the Georgetown Leadership Coaching Program to learn how to support people who wanted to become better leaders.

At Georgetown, it quickly became evident that the principles of yoga—nonjudgment, embracing individuality, not taking oneself too seriously, understanding one right answer doesn't exist, and continuous development and learning—intersected beautifully with the coaching philosophies I was learning. Even so, because I was grappling with self-doubt at the time, I hesitated to integrate these two disciplines into my leadership development work.

While expanding my expertise in yoga and coaching, I took classes in neuroleadership and the psychology of adult development to better understand the science behind the concepts I had learned. I've had a lifelong fascination with studying the brain, which led me to earn a bachelor's degree in psychology. My appreciation for the profound synergy between yoga practices and coaching deepened as I continued to study. Understanding the science of how the brain, body, and breath function led me to develop a holistic approach to leadership development. I tapped into this powerful knowledge and created tools for the executives and senior leaders I support in my coaching practice.

After more than a decade of creating the story in my mind—thinking about it, experiencing the outcomes—I committed to writing this book, drawing from decades of experience as a technology leader, extensive study and practice of yoga and mindfulness, research in neuroscience, and executive coaching. This book synthesizes these diverse influences into an integrated, actionable framework and offers strategies for regaining rest, boosting energy levels, and sharpening mental clarity. Using practical techniques informed by mindfulness and neuroscience, readers can reduce stress, enhance calmness, and improve both physical and mental health. This is a guide to help you embrace the natural functions of your brain, body, and breath, empowering you to elevate your life and leadership with greater ease, confidence, and authenticity.

I've had the honor to serve as an executive coach to CEOs, vice presidents, and directors of private sector companies, United States military generals and colonels, and senior executive officers and leaders of the United States government. Because my coaching experience is working with senior leaders and executives, these will be the stories and examples I use throughout the book. However, the situations, challenges, and opportunities I describe here will apply to anyone—college students, parents, teachers, and workers at all levels.

To my coaching clients over the years—thank you for trusting me as you tackle complex and sometimes extreme leadership challenges and successes. Because confidentiality and trust are at the root of my coaching relationships, I have masked all identities, changing names and organizational leadership positions to ensure confidentiality while telling stories that will help others. At times, my stories are an amalgamation of multiple clients. To my readers, be assured that the clients and positions of responsibility are accurate, and the situations are real.

I also want to make clear that my depictions of events from my childhood, which include a dysfunctional family and neglectful parent, are *my perspective* of what happened to me. Some of my siblings retain memories of a loving, nurturing experience from the same environment. Although we grew up in the same household with the same individuals, how others treated each individual and how we interpreted experiences and retained memories are unique to each of us. Even when they're different, all our stories are true.

When I detail my experience of abuse at the hands of someone I was married to, it is critical to me that readers understand that my current husband, Mark, and the father of my children, Jim, are caring and respectful, and they would never consider physically harming anyone.

May you take the science, stories, and practices to evolve into the best you possible!

CHAPTER 1

MINDFULLY SUCCESSFUL

As a management consulting firm director, my work was rewarding, and the clients were impressive. The CEO, Michael, had a reputation for turning everything he touched to gold. By my measure of success—professional achievement and financial security—he was to be admired.

During a monthly business review meeting with the CEO and other company leaders, I watched Michael berate the vice president as he struggled to present a business plan he had labored on for weeks. Michael insulted and ridiculed the VP. He seemed to enjoy watching him squirm. I was terrified he would call on me.

I wondered: Did Michael think he was being effective? Inspiring? Motivating? He might get the desired deliverable, but at what price? How would it affect the humiliated vice president and everyone in the room who witnessed his behavior?

Experience had taught me that leaders like Michael could make people's lives miserable. I wondered whether perhaps they were just miserable themselves.

Was this CEO doing what I had done for so long? Was he so focused on success that he forgot what it meant to be human?

That meeting reinforced my desire to find a profession that would support leaders—whether it was helping CEOs such as Michael see the impact of their actions, or showing leaders like the VP learn how to respond healthily to a verbal assault.

* * *

Thousands of books are devoted to focused topics: communication, the secret to giving feedback, effective public speaking, or change management, to name a few. Your career path has likely included reading books and taking courses that teach specific skills such as teamwork and collaboration, leadership of virtual and remote teams, effective delegation, and conflict resolution. All these resources can help leaders develop skills, learn techniques, and adjust behavior. But in my decades of experience in the workplace and as an executive coach, they're not sufficient for people to become *mindfully* successful.

What is "mindfully successful"? What does that look like? What does it mean when you're doing something mindfully rather than simply doing something? And why might you even care if you are mindfully successful as long as you're successful?

Being mindful includes acting with awareness of what you are and are not doing and noticing the impact on yourself, others, and the organization which you serve, while not being overly reactive or overwhelmed by what's going on around you. When you reflect on your day, were you fully present in your conversations and activities, or were you already on to the next meeting, topic, or conversation? Were you calm and confident in your approach, or were you inwardly simmering? And are you able to have an objective reflection on your actions of the day, or do you repeatedly replay events, chastising yourself for how you should have done better?

Having extensively studied many disciplines and systems—psychology, anatomy, leadership coaching, philosophy, neuropsychology, and adult development—I have seen that integrating mindfulness into your life can lead to a more profound sense of fulfillment and achievement. By cultivating present-moment awareness and fostering a nonjudgmental attitude, you open yourself to new perspectives, enhancing your capacity for creativity and problem-solving.

Mindful success goes beyond conventional notions of achievement; it involves cultivating emotional intelligence and self-awareness to make conscious choices that align with your core values. By honing these qualities, you can become better attuned to your strengths and weaknesses, enabling you to make informed decisions and forge meaningful paths, and create an environment where innovation and collaboration flourish.

Mindfulness enables you to acknowledge and learn from setbacks, viewing challenges as opportunities for growth and learning and propelling you forward with resilience and adaptability. Moreover, it strengthens your connections with others as you listen more attentively and empathize with colleagues, collaborators, and clients.

I offer this personal guide to help executives and leaders see themselves and use the science of themselves—their brain, their body, and their breath—to become more influential, more effective, and more empowering leaders with greater success.

Sharing what I've learned about being mindfully successful through research, practice, observation, and experience, my goal is to help you see how you can embrace—rather than battle— the functions of your brain and body, as well as employ your breath in ways that will move you through life with greater ease, authenticity, and yes, success.

By contrast, being *mindlessly* successful often includes you, the leader, running on the treadmill of life, working harder and harder, exhausted and exasperated with yourself and others. You might meet the immediate goal, but what negative emotional wake have you left in your quest?

In this ever-changing world, a mindful approach to success empowers you to continuously strive for improvement rather than fixating on perfection.

* * *

Being mindfully successful encompasses multiple parts, including being mindful of what quest for success you are pursuing, as well as acting each day aware of where you are and what you're doing. The journey of mindful success is a lifelong commitment to personal and interpersonal development, empowering you to create a more compassionate and harmonious world for yourself and those around you.

Often people unconsciously define what success means to them based on a child's interpretation of their environment—a large house, lots of money, an important job, happy relationships, or changing the world. An image is placed in their unconscious mind of something they must achieve. Rewarded for being the superstar, a child might have the belief implanted in their mind that to be loved and successful, they must always perform as the superstar. Born into poverty or a less affluent environment, they might believe that they must achieve financial success. Or, growing up in a dysfunctional environment, they might believe they must have the perfect family to be successful.

Set into the road of life, the individual unconsciously carries their definition of success and hones the accompanying skills.

My drive to succeed started when I was young. My earliest memories are growing up in Washington, DC, visiting monuments, statues, and the Smithsonian museums. Signs of greatness were all around. Although our family had little money, our father wanted to expose us to everything the city offered. My ten-year-old brother or twelve-year-old sister would walk with me the three blocks from our apartment to my favorite place to visit, the Library of Congress. I could visit as often as I wanted. Standing in the glorious Great Hall of the Thomas Jefferson Building, which rises seventy-five feet from the marble floor to the stained-glass ceiling, I looked in awe at the millions of books. I wanted to read every single one.

"I want to write a book and get it in here!" thought my four-year-old self, believing (wrongly) that every book published in the United States was housed in that majestic library.

I had seen greatness, and I wanted it.

My blissful childhood ignorance was shattered shortly after my father was diagnosed with advanced lung cancer. In the early 1960s, lung cancer was a death sentence. Not wanting to leave my mother and their six children—aged one to fourteen years old—alone in Washington, DC, my father moved us to Arkansas,

MINDFULLY SUCCESSFUL **5**

where his parents lived. We had no other family or friends in Arkansas. It was the beginning of a lonely existence for me. In addition to missing my friends, I also missed the monuments, statues, and signs of greatness that excited my imagination.

Within a month of arriving in Arkansas, my father died. I was five years old. At my grandparents' house after the funeral, so many people were there. It was noisy, with copious tears and endless stories. Nobody noticed me. I felt small and invisible. As I crouched under the dining room table, feeling very alone in that crowded room, I remember making promises to myself: I would never be dependent on anyone. I would never be left as my mother had been. I would be strong and smart. I would handle everything on my own. Right or wrong, at that moment, I saw my mother as weak and dependent.

So my journey for success had begun, with very definite— yet unconscious—ideas of what success meant: strong, smart, independent, with financial security.

While your story is unique to you, it probably holds a similar impact on defining what success would look like. Mindlessly, without full thought or attention, you set out to achieve your version of success.

Mindfulness begins with awareness and extends to calmly acknowledging and accepting one's feelings and thoughts. Mindfulness can be challenging to embrace because with aware-ness, you might be flooded with self-judgment.

Mind*lessly* successful—working hard and fast to meet some definition of success—leads to being successfully exhausted!

Many people develop their leadership styles based on what had helped them succeed in the past—getting along with others, a laser focus on results, or being adept at office politics or "reading the room." Sometimes they overrely on the one skill they've perfected to address various challenges. The yoga teacher muses, "I just need to meditate more . . ." The academic thinks, "If I understood this theory better . . ." The scientist says, "Explain to me why this is happening . . ." Or the manager says, "It's up to me to find the one right answer."

But as a maxim by world-renowned business educator and leadership coach Dr. Marshall Goldsmith goes: "What got you here won't get you where you want to go."

* * *

As a leader, are you tired of being tired? Weary of people not hearing you, despite consistently repeating yourself? Has your progress been blocked, perhaps by a gap in your understanding— or your best efforts? Does the struggle for success feel more difficult and painful than is necessary for you and those around you? I've been there too.

Turning fifty was a wake-up call for me. I had always perceived myself as thirty-two—whether I was sixteen, twenty-five, forty-two, or approaching fifty. But when my son turned thirty-two, it was like a slap in the face—I was no longer thirty-two. The years had passed.

Around this time, while interviewing for an executive position, the interviewer asked, "When you were a child, what did you want to be when you grew up?" Pausing to think, I replied, "I never really had an idea of what I wanted to be. I've just been fortunate always to find the next position to support the company I worked for and to help me grow." Later, reflecting on the question, I recalled that I had wanted to be an attorney so I could

MINDFULLY SUCCESSFUL   7

help people. Or I wanted to be a scientist so I could figure out how the human body worked.

Forty-five years had passed since I had made a childish vow to be successful. After a twenty-five-year career in the information technology field, I had racked up financial security and plenty of professional accolades.

I was mindlessly successful.

Some internal voice—perhaps brought forth by my yoga practice—told me I could make a much more significant impact by finding a profession that would support leaders and leaders-to-be, like Michael and the vice president he chastised. I realized it was time to make more conscious decisions about my life rather than wait for things to happen and react.

I'd earned a bachelor's degree in psychology but knew I needed more for my next career move. I was accepted into a premier leadership coach training program at Georgetown University. Within a month of completing it, I had my first coaching clients, vice presidents in an information technology consulting company. One client asked why I had become a leadership coach. The answer came without hesitation: "Because I made so many things so much more difficult for myself than they had to be. I want to support others, so their experience won't be as difficult as mine was."

I often wish I had "me" as a coach thirty years ago. Typically, I found a way to succeed at whatever job or responsibility I was given, but looking back, I see that whatever I achieved was much more difficult and painful than was necessary—for me and those around me.

That is the genesis of this book. My hope is to offer lessons to help you achieve and retain success more easily, comfortably, and peacefully than I found mine.

At first glance, the topics this book addresses may seem unrelated, but all leaders share a common denominator—they are all human. They're also humans who have weighty responsibilities with high consequences for failure. Entire books are written about leadership development and related topics, with each expert approaching their domain in depth. But when is a busy executive supposed to have time to read all the books? Take all the workshops? How can you apply what the experts have discovered about brain formation and function to respond more authentically and effectively during leadership challenges and opportunities? How can you use what you've learned about the body on the yoga mat, through health care, or through anatomy books to transform yourself? And how can the science gained about the power of the breath make a difference in your personal power?

You can look at leadership from an integrated approach by figuring out how various domains work together. This book is a guide to help you integrate the science of yourself—your brain, your body, and your breath—to become more influential, more effective, and more empowering. The information offered can help you to achieve greater success with confidence, authenticity, peace, and well-being. Science-based tools and techniques will be outlined to help you change "from the inside out" to help improve your work performance, enhance your leadership ability, and increase your influence on those you lead.

A Road Map

Early in my professional life, I was sure my deep fears, unhealthy reactions, and the recurring (usually negative) stories I told myself were unique. When I began my career as an executive coach, working with top-level leaders in the corporate world and the US government across genders, ages, and backgrounds, I was surprised to discover they had the same challenges, fears, and unhealthy reactions as I had in my career. I saw the same themes and trends emerge again and again, and I became curious.

Each of these senior leaders and executives was already considered "successful"—but at what cost to them and those they were responsible for leading? Exhaustion? Frustration? Missed opportunities? Feelings of not enough? They all had solid business or technical skills and management and leadership training. They incorporated the knowledge they had gained from multiple personality assessments. Although each tool had value, they were working from the outside in. These individuals were "successful," and they were also successfully exhausted.

This book features anecdotes from coaching clients, senior-level executives throughout the world, to illustrate how using the science of the brain, body, and breath has helped them overcome obstacles and attain success mindfully. Through coaching and by utilizing the tools presented in this book, they became *mindfully successful.* The primary thing this book can do for you is to give you science-based information and practical tools to make real change from the inside out. Here are some examples:

- **Recognize and overcome gaps in recognizing.** Susan, a vice president of an international cybersecurity company, was technically brilliant yet struggled with an underlying need to please others. When she began coaching sessions, she was unaware of how this tendency hindered her leadership. Feedback on a 360-assessment stated, "She tries to be everything to everyone instead of holding people accountable," and she "tends to be reactive to events outside her control." Although Susan achieved her company's goals, there was an emotional and physical cost to her, those she led, and her organization. Using brain-training techniques based on neuroplasticity, Susan was able to lead more successfully, with greater ease and more positive impact, and was promoted to senior vice president in her company.

- **Embrace the thinking and feeling brain to promote positive professional moves and personal relationships.** David was a colonel in the US military with global responsibilities. Lives literally depended on his success, and he believed the key to success was emotional detachment. His inability to overcome shame and fear stalled his career, and he was passed over for promotions. Unfortunately, he learned late in his career the repercussions of his actions and was not promoted to general or higher levels of responsibility within the military. However, through our coaching, he learned how to embrace, rather than fight, his emotional brain and became a more effective, inspiring, and peaceful leader, accepting and embracing the leadership positions and opportunities that he had.

- **Calm down and balance yourself with breathing techniques.** Leigh, a management consulting company director, was uncertain how to approach challenging topics with a team of executives as they were headed into a three-day strategic off-site retreat. She felt a high level of distrust among the leaders and worried whether she could have the hard conversations needed to move the company forward. Using breathing techniques allowed her to positively influence key strategic decisions that contributed to the company's growth—and she found the retreat revitalizing and inspiring.

- **Release anxiety with the power of neuroplasticity.** Henry, a US military general, reacted with overwhelming—almost paralyzing—anxiety when he encountered a former boss years after an embarrassing presentation. While he had continued to be promoted since the event, Henry had extreme anxiety whenever the former boss's name was even mentioned. Using techniques to retrain the brain, he was able to release the anxiety and no longer be held emotionally captive to a long-ago event. While the change was not obvious to those he led, the shift within himself was, as he described, "life-changing."

- **Regain rest, increase energy, and think clearly.** Pat, a CEO and majority owner of a $250 million company, was fighting business sabotage from a former partner. When we began coaching, she told me, "I just want to be able to sleep! How do I turn off my brain?" Incorporating breathing techniques allowed her to develop previously untapped resources, which helped her stave off the attempted takeover and expand the business.

Brain, Body, and Breath

This book is based on science. It explains the brain's functions and how neurons can be rewired to change patterns and habits that don't serve you, whether impacting your personal health, professional achievements, or life satisfaction. For example, people often will try to "talk themselves calm" in heated situations, using only the "thinking brain." That is an exercise in futility and frustration because it doesn't account for the "emotional brain." Other facets of brain science addressed include the psychology of meaning-making and neuroleadership, the neurocognitive components underlying complex decision-making and problem-solving processes that leaders face. By understanding how the mind and body work together and by learning to integrate different disciplines and practices into a holistic approach, you can leave behind repeated unhealthy patterns that get in the way of making genuinely life-changing breakthroughs.

The body provides you with infinite information if you're willing to pay attention. But in the drumbeat of daily life, too often its signals are ignored or dismissed. People power through to accomplish what they think needs to be done, sometimes in unhealthy ways. The mind-body connection is relatively new in Western medicine, yet this concept has long been recognized in Eastern medicine. My experience with qigong, developed thousands of years ago as part of traditional Chinese medicine; yoga, developed over five thousand years ago in northern India; and modern Western medicine provide a foundation for an examination of the body's physical functions, particularly the nervous system. Science explains, for example, how body posture can send signals of safety or danger to the brain.

Continuous high-stress levels, whether real or perceived, will hyperactivate your fight-or-flight response, which can result in reactions and behavior not suited to the situation. Meditation, breathwork, and yoga have been shown to be powerful antidotes to stress by activating your "relax-and-renew" response. Several of the techniques in this book can be used to activate or calm the nervous system.

Understanding how the body works, particularly the autonomic nervous system (ANS), can help you achieve your goals mindfully, whether you're trying to get restorative sleep, speak in public, or remain calm in stressful situations. Exercising and managing your autonomic nervous system can help you deal productively with feeling overwhelmed. You can learn to override doubt to project a sense of authentic strength and confidence. Understanding the brain, body, and breath can be helpful anytime you need to lead more effectively. And you can use this information to foster patience and humility.

The breath can be used as a powerful force that integrates the brain and the body. We all breathe, usually without even thinking about it—a human takes 12 to 15 breaths per minute on average. That adds up to 900 breaths per hour and 17,000 per day (some estimates are as high as 17,280–28,800 per day!).

What we often don't realize is that breathing is unique compared to other visceral (e.g., digestion, endocrine, cardiovascular) functions because it can be regulated voluntarily. The behavioral or voluntary control of breathing happens in the brain's cortex, and breathing with conscious control affects the body, such as a self-initiated change in breathing before a vigorous exertion or effort.

While you can't consciously command your heartbeat to slow or your mind to cease chattering, by harnessing the breath, it is possible to make indirect commands to do both. In other words, breathing has a powerful effect on how we feel physically, mentally, and emotionally. In fact, the US military, including the Navy SEALs and air force fighter pilots, use a technique known as "box breathing" in high-stress situations to aid in stress management and overall wellness.

Before my studies, I assumed that tension and stress resulted in shallow breathing or holding my breath. When I felt relaxed, my breathing was slow and even. But I had it backward—the tension was the result of holding my breath or breathing quickly. Breathing fully facilitated calm.

The Integrator

The intent of this book is not to disregard or replace the many skills you have learned through your years of educational or professional experience. Learning about the brain, body, and breath becomes an integrator for leadership.

Working in the technical world of information technology for more than two decades taught me that functionality depends on integration. Regardless of how perfectly the software is developed, the system tested, or the hardware's power, without cohesive integration, the system doesn't function at maximum capacity or efficiency. Though I am experienced in coding, designing, and testing software systems, I lay no claim to being a software (brain) expert. Neither can I assert expertise around the hardware (body) nor communication systems (breath). And I cannot claim to be all users or administrators of the system.

What I offer is considerable study, research, and personal experience. I have extensively studied psychology, anatomy, philosophy, neuropsychology, the nervous system, adult development, and leadership coaching. My lifetime quest has been for knowledge and finding ways to use that knowledge to improve my life. I do the same to help those I coach.

When embraced holistically, these disciplines offer different views of the self. By incorporating all the senses and multiple disciplines, you can learn to be more conscious and become mindfully successful leaders.

As I integrated my lifetime of practices and decades of research, I built a new—and yes, successful—career in executive and leadership coaching. I shifted from trying to identify and solve business problems as a consultant to coaching leaders with wonder, respect, and curiosity. No single right answer exists for anyone. My goal, for more than two decades, has been to introduce and expand leaders' awareness of the brain, body, and breath to help them find the unique answers that are right for them and those they lead.

* * *

Despite the seemingly endless obstacles thrown in my path—childhood poverty, a dysfunctional, neglectful parent, teenage pregnancy, community shunning, a broken back from a car accident, domestic abuse in my previous marriage, gender discrimination and harassment in the workplace, financial struggles, and more, I can say with confidence that I have become mindfully successful. What I know now is that success does not require perfection. Instead, we can learn to look at our imperfections with grace, curiosity, and a willingness to learn rather than chastising or beating ourselves up.

I've found perspective, rather than embarrassment and guilt, when I think about my upbringing, my career, and the life challenges of my younger days. Today, when faced with personal or professional dilemmas, I ask myself, "What would I say to a client?"

Sometimes my friends ask when I'll give up my executive coaching practice. But the truth is, I'm still having fun and making a positive difference. I am still learning and growing. What I do doesn't feel like work. Even so, I know I can't coach the world, and I'm eager to give an expanded audience the benefits of what I've learned about leadership over the years. That's why I am writing this book. I want to offer all leaders specific tools based on the science known about the brain, body, and breath to become more effective, authentic, and healthy. References to the research and science that are the foundation of this book will be included at the end.

To fully benefit from this book, I suggest that you read it in its entirety. The sections are intricately interconnected, and the information and themes covered build on each other. Consider this book as a holistic guide rather than separate parts.

This book is based on the science known today. The experiences are described from my current point of reference. Like Socrates, I encourage every reader to question and consider, "Does this fit? How might it work for me?"

MINDFULLY SUCCESSFUL   17

CHAPTER 2

BRAIN

A brain. We all have one, yet the question remains unanswered—do we control our brain, or does our brain control us? Or does a reciprocal interaction exist between the brain we possess and the actions we undertake?

For much of history, the prevalent belief persisted that the structure and connections of the brain remained relatively unchanging from childhood onward, offering limited potential for growth or alteration in adulthood. This concept of a static brain was widely accepted, likened to the stable structure of one's hand. Sayings like "You can't teach an old dog new tricks" reinforced this viewpoint, implying restricted capacity for learning and adjustment as we get older.

In recent decades, research has powerfully challenged this static view of the brain, and scientists now have compelling evidence that the brain is far more adaptable and malleable than previously believed. Throughout the entire human life span, even into old age, the brain demonstrates an impressive capacity to change and respond to experiences and to the environment. This growing body of research has shed light on the concept of neuroplasticity, which showcases the brain's remarkable ability to rewire and adapt in response to new stimuli, learning, and challenges. This newfound understanding of the brain's potential for growth and transformation not only debunks age-old myths, but it also illuminates an inspiring possibility of continued development and learning and encourages a lifelong pursuit of personal, professional, intellectual, and emotional growth.

As someone who has tended toward skepticism, I've been gratified to see the scientific advances that allow brain activity to be measured and mapped in safe, noninvasive ways. Modern scientists can see how the brain responds to stimuli, which is a far more accurate assessment of brain activity than individuals' often flawed or distorted self-reporting. The more science provides an understanding of how the brain functions, the more easily people can learn to harness its capacities rather than being controlled by them.

Gaining insight into the functioning of the brain has illuminated how I inadvertently hindered my own success. This understanding provided me with the means to rectify these hindrances. In my early career, I held the belief that my profound fears, adverse responses, and recurrent (typically negative) stories I told myself were unique to me. However, my role as an executive coach revealed a striking revelation: a multitude of professionals I assisted, spanning gender, age, background, and occupation, shared comparable fears, responses, and narratives. This unexpected revelation piqued my curiosity profoundly.

For example, anyone who met my clients Henry or Susan (who I mentioned in chapter 1) would likely be resoundingly impressed with their professional accomplishments, their high-level positions, and their overall executive presence.

Henry was a highly successful general in the US military who commanded more than ten thousand people across multinational locations. His expertise was evident in his adeptness at fostering collaborative solutions, innovative strategies, and alliances across varied sectors, including military branches, industry partners, academic institutions, and international associates. Nonetheless, during our coaching sessions, he confided in me about his innate and almost immobilizing anxiety whenever he encountered a former superior. This anxiety stemmed from a pivotal presentation mishap that had haunted him for four years. Despite his subsequent ascension through the ranks, numerous accolades, and widespread acclaim, the mere mention of that individual's name triggered a distressing spiral in his mindset, even though he no longer reported to this former boss.

Susan, a senior vice president at an international cybersecurity company, struggled with the feedback on a 360-assessment that questioned her leadership style. Her colleagues said, "She tries to be everything to everyone instead of holding people accountable" and "She tends to be reactive to events outside her control." When we began our coaching sessions, she was unaware of the ways this underlying tendency to please others hindered her leadership. She saw herself as successful because she always had been able to meet her company's goals. But as we explored the feedback, she began to realize her achievement came at a high cost to her, those she led, and her organization.

Both executives, like countless others, were being unconsciously controlled by neural pathways formed in their brains. For Susan, the neural pathways were formed over decades. For

Henry, the neural pathway was ingrained by a single traumatic event. For many others (including me), neural pathways are formed from a single traumatic childhood event and become reinforced throughout the years.

Does this mean that Susan, Henry, countless others, and I are doomed to be victims of our pasts? Thanks to what we're learning from science, the answer is a resounding "No!"

Neurons are the longest-living cells in our bodies and comprise the brain's communication system. Neuron cells are like a delivery service, carrying information from the brain to other organs and the rest of the body. Neural pathways help speed communication, creating shortcuts encoded by our experiences, like grooves on a vinyl record. Once the needle starts playing a record, it predictably follows the established groove. But just like a vinyl record can be scratched, which creates a new path for the needle, the brain's patterns also can be interrupted. You can learn to create different neural pathways that can break down barriers to success and create more productive actions and habits.

The work of psychologist Donald Hebb, considered the father of neuropsychology, merged the psychological and neuroscience worlds. The phrase "Neurons that fire together wire together" is attributed to him. When mammals think or act, the brain's neurons fire, and with repeated firing, thoughts and actions are "carved" into your brain, eventually creating a path of least resistance in your reactions and behaviors. Just as the words and the music on an album vinyl groove don't change, you repeatedly react in the same ways, even though sometimes your actions and thoughts are not healthy or no longer serve you.

You can become alert to the ways that unhealthy fear and reactions drive your behavior, including tuning into and training your emotional brain, called the limbic system. For example, the amygdala, housed in the limbic system, is designed to be hyper-vigilant and make instantaneous judgments to determine what is safe versus what could be dangerous. The amygdala's primary job is valuable—to help humans survive—but it can also distort our interpretation of and reaction to events. Thanks to science, we now have proven methods to harness the amygdala rather than letting it control us.

Other instinctual thought patterns that can create obstacles to mindful success include the "monkey mind," a Buddhist term that describes the unsettled, restless, confused thoughts and worries that swirl in your consciousness. By exercising the "feeling brain" rather than relying solely on the "thinking brain," you can train the restless mind to settle down and become calmer.

I'm not saying these kinds of changes are easy. Change is inherently difficult. But with time and effort, science has shown us that by "rewiring our brains," new neural pathways can support positive responses to change for better, more successful results.

The knowledge about the brain presented here is rooted in scientific findings and encompasses well-established practices and actionable advice. This information equips you to effect positive transformations. Armed with knowledge, comprehension, and practical application, you can enhance your capabilities, enabling you to lead more adeptly, mitigate internal conflicts, and attain success in both professional and personal realms with greater serenity and satisfaction. This insight resonates with various challenges I've encountered within myself and the recurring patterns I've observed in the lives of my clients.

A Closer Look at the Brain

Theories and speculation about the brain's function and processing have fascinated humans for centuries. As early as 460 to 379 BC, humans documented their curiosity about the brain, as demonstrated by Hippocrates's observation that the brain is the seat of intelligence. In 387 BC, Plato echoed that observation about the organ's role in the mental process. And as early as 280 BC, Erasistratus of Chios had noted distinct divisions in the brain.

The adult brain, often described as a "blob of fat," weighs about three pounds and is composed of fat, water, protein, carbohydrates, and salts. The description doesn't sound impressive, yet the blood vessels and nerves that run throughout the brain's tissue are literally the control center for the entire body's system and functions.

People typically equate the brain with thinking. They interchange the words "brain," "mind," and "consciousness," but each is discrete and distinct. Understanding the distinctions between brain, mind, and thought helps you understand that *you* are in the driver's seat of your reactions and responses to life. Nothing about the brain requires you to be a victim of your history or a passive participant in your future.

The medical community learned much about the brain's influence on personality from a bizarre accident involving Phineas Gage, a twenty-five-year-old American railroad construction foreman in Cavendish, Vermont. In 1848, Gage became famous as "the man who survived an iron bar passing through his head" (more precisely, his frontal lobes). Gage is a fixture in the curricula of neurology, psychology, and neuroscience, and he has been called one of "the great medical curiosities of all time."[*]

---

[*] Macmillan, Malcolm, "Inhibition and Phineas Gage: Repression and Sigmund Freud," *Neuropsychoanalysis* 6, no. 2 (2004): 181–92.

Gage was using a tamping iron—43 inches long, 1.25 inches in diameter, and weighing 13.25 pounds—to pack explosive powder into a hole. When the powder detonated, the tamping iron shot upward, entering Gage's left cheek, ripping through his brain, and exiting through the top of his skull. He is said to have not even lost consciousness. Other than the entry and exit wounds and the loss of his left eye, he had no other apparent physical damage. He became a medical celebrity.

Dr. John Martyn Harlow, who treated Gage for a few months afterward, noted that his external physical functions appeared unchanged. However, the regulation between his "intellectual faculties and animal propensities" seemed to be gone. Harlow wrote that Gage could not stick to plans, uttered "the grossest profanity," and showed "little deference for his fellows." Gage's friends found him "no longer Gage." Before the accident, Gage was considered a model foreman. After the accident, his former employer refused to take him back. After a series of odd jobs— working in a stable in New Hampshire, driving coaches in Chile—Gage eventually joined relatives in San Francisco, where he died in May 1860 at age thirty-six after a series of seizures.*

Considering such a severe brain injury, why were the physical effects so minimal and the personality changes so profound? Doctors wondered whether the brain's segments affected different functions. Could one part of the brain affect personality, while another controlled physical functions?

Although there is archeological evidence that human skulls had holes drilled into them seven thousand to ten thousand years

---

* Steve Twomey, "Phineas Gage: Neuroscience's Most Famous Patient," *Smithsonian Magazine*, November 15, 2013, https://www.smithsonianmag.com/history/phineas-gage-neurosciences-most-famous-patient-11390067/.

ago, until recently, most of what was known about brains was based on observation and studying the brains from corpses. The "fat blob" has long kept many secrets about what was happening amid the wrinkles.

In 1900, Harvey Cushing, considered the father of neuro-surgery, performed the first successful brain tumor operations. In 1929, German scientists published the first study using an electroencephalograph (EEG), which measures and records brain-wave patterns, allowing scientists to observe the brain's activity levels and trace connections between one part of the central nervous system and another.

Functional magnetic resonance imaging (fMRI), intro-duced in the early 1990s, further revolutionized the study of how the brain functions. The technology allows scientists to study brain activity without damaging brain cells, to locate brain activity more precisely, and to map what stimuli activate specific brain regions.

Combining fMRI, which measures blood flow changes to specific brain regions, and EEG, which measures electrical activity, provides neuroscientists with extensive information on what is happening in areas of brain activity and how one reacts in the moment to different experiences.

Our Three Brains

Neuroscientist Dr. Paul MacLean introduced the concept of the "triune brain" in the 1960s, which describes three distinct layers of the mammalian brain—the *body brain*, the *thinking brain*, and the *emotional brain*. While many in neuroscience today find the three-brain model oversimplified, for the layperson, its simplicity can help illustrate the effects of each layer in human behavior, especially in the relationship between cognition and emotion.

For day-to-day functions, it is unnecessary to remember what area of the brain controls specific activities. Instead, it can be helpful to visualize the brain's organization and structure.

For the purposes of this book, we focus mostly on the *thinking brain* and *emotional brain*. While the cerebrum is involved in functions such as thinking and reasoning, the discussion of the brain wouldn't be complete without the cerebellum, often referred to as the *body brain*. The cerebellum is a small section of the brain, yet it holds more than half of the neurons in your whole body. Small but mighty, the cerebellum literally keeps us straight—it regulates motor control and learning, coordinates voluntary movements, balance, and posture.

The cerebral cortex, often called the *thinking brain*, regulates higher-order conscious activity, such as thought processing and action. It might be viewed as the outer wrap of the brain and is generally referenced by the lobes depicted below.

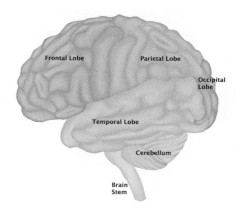

THE THINKING BRAIN

The frontal lobe, at the front of the cerebral cortex, comprises the brain's largest area and drives expressive language, reasoning, higher-level cognition, and motor skills. This is where logical and abstract thought, language, creativity, and working memory reside. When we "think about thinking," the frontal lobe lights up, hence, the thinking brain. The prefrontal cortex, a part of the frontal lobe, regulates and manages emotional and social behavior. (The prefrontal cortex in Phineas Gage's brain was damaged by the railroad iron, which explains his behavioral changes.)

Tactile senses such as pain, pressure, and touch are processed in the *parietal lobe*; information sent from the eyes is processed in the *occipital lobe*; and memory formation and processing sounds being recorded by the ears happen in the *temporal lobe*.

Typically, each of the brain's four lobes is represented on each hemisphere of the brain. The hemispheres are connected by the corpus callosum, which delivers messages from one half of the brain to the other.

Scientists now know that most brain functions rely on many different areas working together across the neural network; however, each lobe carries out most functions as described above.

Underneath the lobes of the thinking brain lies the limbic system, often referred to as the *emotional brain* or the *feeling brain*. The limbic system plays a critical role in our emotional and behavioral responses, and it is where the amygdala resides.

LIMBIC SYSTEM

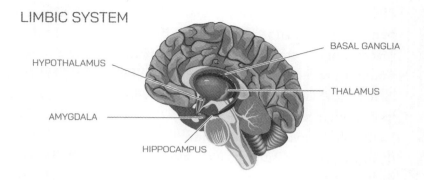

THE EMOTIONAL BRAIN

The *amygdala*, a walnut-sized portion of the limbic system, is like an emotional sentry. It is the first responder to external stimuli (an encounter, a sound, or an event) and initiates the "fight, flight, or freeze" response. Its primary job is to determine the level of danger being posed to you.

The amygdala gets a lot of attention, but other parts of the limbic system also play vital roles. Can't sleep? Stress eating? Hormones out of whack? That's also your emotional brain—specifically the *hypothalamus*—at work.

Is stress making you feel less sharp or high performing? That's the function of the *hippocampus*, which helps in learning and memory building. Sitting at the top of the limbic system, the thalamus is the central relay station for all information (except for smell) before being transferred to the thinking brain (cerebral cortex) for processing.

Working Together

The brain—as we understand it now—is more accurately defined by areas rather than separate entities. Neurons, the nerve cells that transmit information to other cells, control these areas. The thinking brain (cerebral cortex), the emotional brain (limbic system), and the cerebellum (body brain) constantly and seamlessly work together.

Memory serves as a prime illustration of brain regions functioning in harmony. Although memory storage is frequently linked to the hippocampus, the amygdala in the emotional brain and the neocortex in the thinking brain collaborate in crafting, storing, and recalling memories. Picturing the distinct brain areas—the thinking brain and emotional brain—can aid in boosting your brain awareness while practicing mindfulness and meditation.

Just as memories rely on different brain areas, so do your thoughts, actions, and reactions. For example, the frontal cortex (thinking brain) is instrumental in driving *emotional behavior*, but the limbic system (emotional brain) determines how you interpret events or other stimuli, thus identifying the *emotional response* to an event.

The amygdala is essential to human survival. If you had to logically process "safe or danger" in every circumstance, you might be dead or injured before the thought had time to form in the frontal lobe. When you see, hear, touch, or taste something, the amygdala classifies the event as safety or danger, which quickly resonates through the limbic system before it gets to the cortex—the thinking brain—for action. In other words, we receive input, "safe" or "danger," which triggers "fight, flight, or freeze." The *emotional brain* gets the first crack at information before being moved to the cortex, or the *thinking brain*.

The amygdala, designed to protect early humans from life-threatening dangers, doesn't always serve optimally in the modern world, where hypervigilance can become a hindrance. Is an unexpected encounter with your boss, like Henry experienced, truly life-threatening? If not, why does the amygdala still trigger danger signals that lead to fight, flight, or freeze responses?

In situations perceived as emergencies, the amygdala can take control of the brain, a common occurrence. For example, unexpectedly encountering your boss, making a mistake, or running late for a crucial meeting can trigger an "amygdala hijack." These snap judgments can be lifesaving, yet they can also lead to hasty, extreme, or mistaken assessments, negatively impacting you and those around you. When your boss critiques your work, you might react defensively. An aggressive driver cutting you off might spark anger. A comment from a colleague could result in a harsh response. Or sudden, unexplained fear might overwhelm you.

These instances signify an amygdala hijack where emotions are commandeered. Understanding these brain processes empowers you to take charge of your reactions, rather than feeling powerless in your own life. Recognizing this tendency to over-judge enables you to significantly reduce unnecessary stress for yourself and others.

Early events in my life resulted in my amygdala being overly sensitive to illness and abandonment. My life experiences sent faulty interpretations to my thinking brain, for example, and I often sensed danger when none existed, reacting to events in ways that didn't serve me. My earliest awareness of this over-sensitivity happened as I walked down the hall to my therapist's office. I realized that each time I approached his door,

BRAIN **31**

I expected his nameplate to be removed. A piece of me (my amygdala) had prepared me for abandonment. I truly expected that he might have moved since my last visit and neglected to tell me. That insight made for an interesting—and valuable—therapy session.

Understanding that the amygdala's signals should be vetted (after all, it's a small, primitive part of the whole brain) is the first step toward training yourself to stop reacting instinctively. You can check those first impulses to yell, to become defensive, or to retreat. With time and practice, you can recalibrate the safety/fear measure within the amygdala.

> The emotional brain gets first dibs on information before it's transmitted to the thinking brain. That's why *thinking* yourself calm won't work.

That's why *thinking* yourself calm isn't effective—that is working from the outside in. Your brain works from the inside out. No matter how smart or educated you are, the emotional brain gets first dibs on information processing before it's transmitted to the thinking brain. Left unchecked, the emotional brain's quick judgment can steer you in the wrong direction.

On the other hand, it's important not to overrely on the thinking brain. Many executives I coach proudly declare themselves divorced from emotions and want to rely solely on their thinking brains.

"I don't do emotions," a new CEO that I had begun coaching proudly stated.

"I see the world through facts, not emotion," another client told me. "It is a sign of maturity and professionalism."

I could relate. For many years I, too, believed emotion had no place in the professional world. Be smart, use logic, work hard. My default operating system was to rely solely on intellect to find answers.

However, the emotional brain is an integral part of the human experience that shapes our feelings and responses. Denying emotions' existence does not make them disappear; instead, it may lead them to surface in harmful, uncontrollable ways. Relying solely on the thinking brain or intellect overlooks essential aspects of being. Just as you study to enhance intellectual capacity and work out to strengthen physical fitness, tending to your emotional brain cultivates authentic leadership and personal growth. Unraveling the inner workings of the emotional brain paves the way for greater effectiveness and fulfillment as leaders.

Distinction between the Brain, Mind, and Thoughts

As mentioned earlier, the brain, the mind, and our thoughts have fascinating distinctions.

The **brain**, nestled in our skulls, has a defined structure and shape that can be touched, measured, and weighed. It serves as the biological command center of our bodies. With its awe-inspiring network of blood vessels, nerve cells, neurons, synapses, and neurotransmitters, it orchestrates our bodily functions and processes sensory information. The brain plays a pivotal role in shaping our experiences and responses, but it is not synonymous with the mind.

The **mind** is an abstract concept used to characterize thoughts, feelings, subjective states, and self-awareness. An ever-evolving tapestry of consciousness, the mind's exquisite interplay of thoughts, emotions, and perceptions shape our sense of self and understanding of the world. In this way, it goes beyond mere neural activities; it encompasses intangible aspects of consciousness and self-awareness. It is responsible for desires, motives, and choices.

Thoughts are the products of the mind—the mental representations and interpretations of experience. Neuroscientists believe that thoughts are an effect of firing neurons, creating an ever-flowing stream of ideas and concepts that arise from cognitive functioning, often referred to as "conscious cognitive processes."

When the "monkey mind" was referenced earlier, it was not implying that one's brain was physically shaped like a monkey, but rather that the mind—the shapeless, unstructured compilation of a person's understanding and thought processes—was jumping about wildly.

The distinctions and interplay of the brain, the mind, and thoughts can give you valuable insights into the complexities of human cognition and the potential for personal growth and transformation. Understanding opens the door to cultivating greater self-awareness, challenging limiting beliefs, and expanding your cognitive capacities to navigate the intricacies of life with enhanced wisdom and resilience.

Using fMRI, scientists can measure brain activity as people think of different events and determine which parts of the brain "fire." Studies show that thinking about an activity emits the same neural response as the activity. As reported in the

Wu Tsai Neurosciences Institute at Stanford University, the motor cortex—the part of the brain primarily responsible for movement—shows activity when a person imagines hitting a tennis ball, even when the person is lying completely still. And scientists see activity in the hippocampus, responsible for memory and spatial navigation, when a person imagines walking through their house.*

Acknowledging the power of your thoughts can be pivotal in modifying your brain activity and, subsequently, your mind. Incessantly worrying that something undesirable might happen can have the same physical impact as if the event occurred. By changing your thoughts, which you have conscious control over, you can rewire your brain and change your mind.

> With attention, you can control or direct
> your thoughts, which influence your
> mind and can alter your brain.

Why does this matter? Because with attention, controlling or directing your thoughts influences your mind and can alter your brain. Without conscious effort, your thoughts will take the path of least resistance, which results in mindlessly repeating negative behaviors and reactions.

---

* Kelly Zalocusky, "NeuWrite West—Ask a Neuroscientist: Thinking beyond the Halle Berry Neuron," NeuWrite West, April 28, 2015, https://www.neuwritewest.org/blog/2015/4/28/beyond-halle-berry.

Learned Behaviors— Ingraining the Pathways

Learned behaviors can be the result of either conscious or unconscious learning. By shedding light on how you developed behaviors, habits, and fears, you can better navigate and retrain your brain to produce more desirable, mindful outcomes.

Conscious learning is when a person intentionally enters an activity for the purpose of learning new skills or insights, such as listening to a lecture or reading instructions. **Unconscious learning** is rooted in our repeated experiences and social interactions and influences how we perceive the world and interact with others in complex ways.

Some unconscious learning is positive and healthy, such as children who learn kindness, compassion, generosity, and healthy problem-solving skills by watching adults exhibit such behaviors. However, unconscious learning can also have a long-lasting negative impact on humans if they don't become aware of the root cause of their behaviors and beliefs.

In fact, different parts of the brain are responsible for conscious and unconscious learning processes.

The neocortex, the outer layer of the brain, plays a significant role in conscious learning. This part of the brain is associated with higher-order cognitive functions, such as conscious awareness, thinking, reasoning, and decision-making. When you consciously learn something, like a new skill or a piece of information, the neocortex processes and stores this knowledge. This type of learning involves deliberate attention and effort, and you're aware of the learning process taking place.

The basal ganglia, a group of nuclei located deep within the brain, primarily in the forebrain region, and the cerebellum are two areas of the brain that are involved in unconscious or implicit learning. Unconscious learning can have a greater impact on you because it is rarely questioned—it's just the way things are. While you might recall when you learned specific skills or information, without great awareness, you may remain oblivious to the root of your beliefs and behaviors that you acquired without consciousness.

In summary, different parts of the brain are specialized for various types of learning. Conscious learning involves the neocortex, while unconscious learning involves the basal ganglia and cerebellum. These brain regions work together to enable a wide range of learning experiences, both conscious and unconscious.

One form of unconscious learning, fear conditioning, holds a significant place in human psychology.

For researchers, fear conditioning, which involves linking a neutral stimulus to a negative or aversive event resulting in the emergence of fear or anxiety, serves as a treasure trove of valuable insights into psychology, neuroscience, and behavior. It unravels the fundamental mechanisms of learning, delves into the neurobiological underpinnings of fear, provides valuable insights into anxiety disorders, aids in the development of effective behavioral therapies, and sheds light on the intricate processes of memory and cognition. By exploring fear conditioning, scientists gain a deeper understanding of how our minds form associations and emotional responses, unlocking potential avenues for addressing fears and anxieties to improve mental well-being.

To comprehend how you can become the best version of yourself, it is helpful to understand how you became the current version. Delving into unconscious learning can unlock mysteries hidden within yourself.

Unconscious learning has been thoroughly investigated in controlled experiments. Three pivotal studies—Pavlov's dogs, the Little Albert experiment, and Mary Cover Jones's desensitization research—have added significant understanding to how fears and phobias are acquired and how emotional responses can be conditioned. They've influenced behavior therapy for anxiety disorders, introducing techniques like exposure therapy and desensitization. These studies underscore human development's adaptability and the capacity to undo conditioned learning.

Physiologist Ivan Pavlov, in the late nineteenth century, conducted experiments in which he paired a neutral stimulus (a bell) with an unconditioned stimulus (food) that naturally elicited a response (salivation from dogs). After several repetitions of this pairing, the bell alone started to evoke a salivary response, even without the presence of food.

In 1919, psychologist John Watson conducted an experiment on a nine-month-old infant (now considered highly unethical), referred to as Little Albert. While the method deserves condemnation, what Watson learned has become etched in psychology as evidence of classical conditioning: the association of a particular stimulus or behavior with an unrelated stimulus or behavior. Scientists say that babies enter the world with only two fears: loud noises and falling. In the infamous experiment, Watson and an associate, Rosalie Rayner, tested the theory that humans had a collection of unlearned emotions—including fear—that could be taught. In the experiment, Little Albert was shown several objects: a white rat, monkey, dog, and rabbit masks, and the infant showed no fear. Watson then showed the white rat (neutral stimulus) accompanied by striking a hammer on a steel bar behind Little Albert's head, using the notion that loud noises are one of two fears with which infants are born.

Over time, Little Albert became conditioned to fear the rat, even when it was not accompanied by the loud noise, and became fearful of other furry animals. Watson's intent was to continue the experiment to show that fears could be desensitized, but Little Albert's mother withdrew him from the hospital before desensitization could be tested.

While Watson conducted experiments to instill fear, Mary Cover Jones's study was one of the earliest attempts to remove or reduce fears using the same psychological principles. Jones worked with a three-year-old boy named Peter, who had developed a fear of rabbits. Peter's fear was so strong that he would cry and show signs of distress whenever he encountered a rabbit or even a rabbitlike image, such as a drawing.

Using principles of classical conditioning, Jones set out to desensitize Peter's fear response. She started by presenting Peter with a rabbit at a distance where he felt comfortable and gradually moved the rabbit closer while ensuring that Peter remained calm and relaxed. She also paired the presence of the rabbit with positive stimuli, such as food and toys, to create a positive association. Over time, through systematic exposure and positive reinforcement, Peter's fear of rabbits diminished significantly.

* * *

Your life has been a series of events, some of which have etched fear into your brain—fear of rejection, fear of public speaking, fear of failure—to name a few. Since infants are only born with two fears—loud noises and falling—where did your other fears originate? Some are healthy, such as fear of standing in heavy traffic, fear of guns, fear of falling. But what about the less obvious (or useful) fears that control your daily life?

It is possible to nurture and train your emotional brain and to unlearn unhealthy fears. Science has shown that humans can change the neural pathways in their brains by changing their conscious thoughts. This is defined as neuroplasticity, also known as neural plasticity or brain plasticity, a process that involves adaptive structural and functional changes to the brain.* Simply put, neuroplasticity is the ability to change the natural reactions within our brains.

The Power of Neuroplasticity

Popeye the Sailor Man said, "I yam what I yam." Like Popeye, when talking about their attributes or characteristics, many of the clients I work with say, "This is just who I am. It's how I've always been." Often, they say it to justify why they haven't made desired changes—they can't change how they react, how they behave, or what they think because they are who they are. The science of neuroplasticity shatters the notion of being stuck in our ways. It reveals that with consistent, conscious effort, you possess the ability to reshape your reactive thoughts and behaviors. Your brain is adaptable and capable of rewiring to break free from unhealthy learned patterns.

Recall when you learned a new skill, like driving. Initially, your brain's neurons lacked a seamless connection for steering,

---

* Matt Puderbaugh and Prabhu D. Emmady, "Neuroplasticity," StatPearls Publishing, updated May 8, 2022, https://www.ncbi.nlm.nih.gov/books/NBK557811/.

accelerating, and watching the road simultaneously. Operating the vehicle and staying on course demanded conscious, deliberate thought. In this learning phase, your brain and the message-transmitting neurons were in overdrive, filtering every sight and sound through your limbic system to gauge safety. Neurons within the occipital lobe interpreted visuals, the parietal lobe engaged in steering, and the frontal lobe ignited for advanced cognition, reasoning, and motor skills. As you practiced, neurons fired repeatedly, forging connections. Eventually, starting the ignition and driving became innate, and you've likely zoned out while driving without realizing it.

Just as one's brain can adapt and make changes with repeated physical patterns such as driving an automobile, neuroplasticity can be fostered through thoughts and mental exercises.

Researchers using fMRI have documented brain rewiring in athletes mastering specific movements or skills repeatedly. These studies underscore how intensive practice triggers structural and functional brain changes, fostering expertise.

One research study by Naomi Eisenberger and Matthew Lieberman, PhD, of the Department of Psychology, UCLA, showed that the pain sensors in the brain are activated by *thinking* about pain.* In other words, your brain responds to thinking about events as much as doing, seeing, or feeling them.

Habit formation is another compelling showcase of neuroplasticity's power. Habits are routines executed automatically, requiring minimal conscious effort. Every time you engage in an activity, linked neural circuits in your brain strengthen their connections, creating a smoother route.

---

* *Trends in Cognitive Sciences* 8, no. 7 (July 2004).

Whether the activity you repeatedly engage in is to worry or to engage in creative thinking, through repeated exposure and reinforcement, these neural pathways become stronger and create a new "path of least resistance."

> **COACHING DISCLAIMER:** Coaching is about looking forward and growing; therapy is looking backward and healing. As a coach, I do not lead my clients through their past to help heal. Still, understanding neuroplasticity, I may explore the formation of their thought patterns so they can shift their brains' paths of least resistance and develop healthier responses and skills.

When I first began coaching Susan, who struggled with an underlying need to please, she was despondent about the culture survey her organization had conducted. "How do I deal with some of the things that were said about me?" she asked. "This one comment specifically called me out by name." As she reviewed the feedback with me, she was fixated on one sentence.

Not surprisingly, she was interpreting the feedback very personally—her name was attached—and the comments lit up neural pathways that had been embedded throughout her brain for almost fifty years.

During our sessions, she revealed that making everyone happy was extremely important. "It's really important to keep harmony," she said.

42 MINDFULLY SUCCESSFUL

I asked about her past and what it was like for her growing up.

While defending her father ("He was a good father but not the best dad"), she said he had been controlling and isolating. Friends weren't allowed in their house. She watched as her mother, once magnetic and engaged, became withdrawn. During Susan's college years, her father disowned her because he disagreed with the field of study she chose. "I remember that night so vividly," she said as she recounted events that had taken place more than thirty years earlier.

As we explored how these beliefs were formed, Susan realized that she had spent her entire life with the reinforcing belief that to be safe—in her home, her work, and her relationships—it was paramount to keep harmony. "I'd never thought of it that way," she said after a bit of reflective silence. We agreed that because the painful conditioning was so deep, she had considerable healing to do. We suspended our coaching engagement—which is forward-looking for growth—to give her time to look backward and heal through therapy.

When neural pathways carved over decades are coupled with traumatic or highly stressful events, the pathways are even more deeply etched. Susan's instinct to keep harmony in interpersonal relationships sprang from years of repeated reinforcement from her father, which was underscored by the trauma of being disowned because of a seemingly safe decision of choosing a college major.

Without conscious effort, your thoughts will continue to take the path of least resistance, sometimes resulting in repeating negative behaviors and reactions. Science has shown that humans can change the brain's neural pathways by changing conscious thoughts. With repeated and focused attention, you can control or direct thoughts and alter your brain.

Thoughts are more than just fleeting energetic blips; they have the power to continue reinforcing reactions and behaviors that do not serve you, as well as give you the fuel to change your brain's neural pathways.

Simply put, neuroplasticity is the ability to change the natural reactions within our brains, and science has shown that humans are able to make changes by altering their thoughts.

Quick to Judge

If you're walking down the street in the early evening dusk and see a figure approaching, without conscious thought, your brain immediately determines whether you are in danger or safe. You adjust your behavior accordingly. Likewise, when you meet a new client or colleague, you sum up whether they are trustworthy and determine how much of yourself—and your work—to reveal. You make constant, immediate judgments about your environment, both consciously and unconsciously. The brain is geared to judge—its role provides an inherent survival instinct, particularly the amygdala, whose job is to keep us safe.

However, humans can be slow to exercise discernment in their judgments. They are often hypervigilant in passing judgments, with the harshest judgments reserved for themselves. Given the deep roots of this judgmental instinct, it can be beneficial to manage excessive judgmental tendencies while retaining their constructive aspects.

We've discussed the brain's role in making rapid judgments for safety and danger. It's also wired for efficiency and is excellent at recognizing patterns based on past experience. Relying on mental shortcuts, or heuristics, helps you make quick decisions rather

44 MINDFULLY SUCCESSFUL

than engaging in exhaustive analysis. Add in social dynamics that have evolved as a way to build and maintain relationships and cultural and environmental factors that can influence the speed and content of judgments, and it would be easy to believe that humans more often unconsciously react rather than consciously act.

Many cognitive processes underlie human judgment. While quick judgments can be helpful in many situations, they also can lead to biases and errors. Understanding these processes can help people become more aware of their biases and make more informed and fair judgments.

Shirzad Chamine, author of the bestselling book *Positive Intelligence*, describes ten saboteurs, or "internal enemies . . . a set of automatic and habitual mind patterns, each with its own voice, beliefs, and assumptions that work against your best interest."[*] Chamine describes "The Judge" as the master saboteur, compelling one "to constantly find faults with yourself, others, and your conditions and circumstances."

Comprehending the multifaceted cognitive processes underlying human judgment provides individuals with the vital tools to become aware of their own biases and cognitive limitations. Awareness empowers you to actively mitigate the impact of cognitive biases, emotions, and external influences on decision-making processes. Ultimately, this leads to more accurate, just, and considered judgments in various aspects of life—including the messages you tell yourself about yourself.

How can you become more aware? How can you create a practice to notice what is happening and observe your actions and reactions?

---

[*]   Shirzad Chamine, *Positive Intelligence* (Austin, Texas: Greenleaf Book Group Press, 2012).

Perception → Recognition → Action

With your intertwined thoughts and mind, the perception → recognition → action process is a dynamic and ongoing cycle central to navigating and interacting with your surroundings. This process, depicted below, plays a crucial role in many everyday activities, from simple tasks like picking up a cup to complex behaviors such as driving a car or playing a musical instrument. This process is also instrumental to how humans respond to and interact with themselves and others.

The first step is to perceive a sensory experience around you—this is **perception**. It includes recognizing the stimulus and your actions in response to that stimulus. Perception creates our experience of the world.

After we perceive a stimulus, the brain quickly categorizes and interprets what you are sensing and gives meaning to the object—this is **recognition**. This function must happen quickly—can you imagine if you had to slowly and consciously interpret and reinterpret every stimulus that you encountered? By placing objects in meaningful categories (e.g., good, bad, safe, harmful, etc.), you can quickly understand and respond.

The third step of the process involves **action** (or inaction) in response to the stimuli—running from danger, joyful laughter, shooing a fly away, or moving on to the next stimuli.

Your body and mind go through the perception → recognition → action process millions and millions of times daily.

1. Perception
Detecting information from our environment: What you see, hear, touch, taste, and smell. Your brain quickly processes the data received including identifying shapes, colors, etc.

3. Action
Decision-making, motor planning, and execution. Closely linked to perception, we now make decisions about how to respond.

2. Recognition
The brain integrates the basic sensory information and interprets their significance. Higher-level cognitive processes such as memory and attention may be engaged to interpret the recognized information.

What occurs when, throughout the day, you consistently rush through this process, essentially operating on autopilot? You might see this as being intelligent, fast, and well-practiced. However, this often means your reactions are based on preestablished categories, past experiences that could be irrelevant, and ingrained habits in thinking.

When you understand the potentially negative consequences of taking careless or counterproductive actions, you can alter beliefs, adopt practices, and create new, more productive habits.

Alexander Caillet, CEO and cofounder of Corentus, a Boston-based organizational consulting and coaching firm, developed a model called "the Thinking Path," based on the premise that *thought* is at the base of our moment-to-moment reality.* Thoughts lead to feelings, behaviors, and ultimately, results.

---

* Janice Caillet, "The Thinking Path—Corentus," Corentus, August 31, 2023, https://corentus.com/blog/the-thinking-path.

My clients and I have found both Chamine's and Caillet's models to be highly effective and helpful. They rely on noticing during the late recognition and early action phases described in the above graphic.

By exercising your brain in the earlier phase of perception/recognition/action, you can increase or reduce the conscious energy required by you as you interact with your environment and increase efficiency. (Don't worry—the amygdala, which is designed to keep you safe, will still be doing its essential function as it is primarily engaged in the early perception phase.)

Noticing or Judging?

Matt, a senior executive in a management consulting firm, believed his hypervigilance was essential to his long climb up the corporate ladder. To be anything less than high alert would amount to letting his guard down and falling fast. While the high-alert state had benefits, such as recognizing challenges and opportunities others missed, it also resulted in him being highly critical of himself and others. Some people saw this as arrogance, but inside, he was constantly fighting to be good enough.

In a coaching session, he was lamenting about the inefficient, stupid, and ineffective people he constantly dealt with (including himself). I asked if he could describe one of them using only data that could be verified. He began describing his colleague as, "He's kind of tall, fairly good look, trim, probably one of the brightest on my team." I asked him how many of those descriptors—tall, good-looking, trim, bright—could be quantified. Dumbfounded, he looked at me and exclaimed, "What does it matter?"

The problem wasn't that Matt wasn't noticing. He was

noticing with the intention of making a rapid judgment—was this person or event good or bad? Would a situation help or hurt him in his personal pursuit? In the rush to judge, people often do not capture the true sense of *awareness* of what is happening—what exactly are they doing or not doing? When do these events occur? Are you interpreting the perception solely through the lens of past experiences, or are you allowing for fresh data?

Imagine if you could train your brain to be conscious in your recognition, thus producing actions that better serve you and your needs.

I asked Matt to observe the room in which we were meeting and describe it using quantifiable information. The purpose was to bring awareness to his noticing so that he would interrupt the rapid process between perception and recognition. At first, Matt had trouble describing the room: "It's a small, warm room, not too much furniture . . ." I interrupted. How did he measure small, warm, or not too much?

Do you notice that every description was a judgment? I asked him to try describing it again using only facts, not judgment. That was more difficult.

"Oh right. It's probably a fifteen-by-twenty-foot rectangular-shaped room," he began. "It's about seventy-four degrees Fahrenheit . . ." And on he continued, noticing each time he made an assessment, which is based on judgment, versus an assertion, which is quantifiable. He continued slowly, first seeming frustrated, eventually finding humor, and finally laughing at the effort he was expending.

I invited Matt to do the Noticing exercise, described below, for five minutes daily for the next two weeks and report back on what, if any, changes he observed in his thoughts or behavior.

BRAIN **49**

Training the Brain

Consistent "brain training" can help you change the unconscious path of least resistance, based on your history, to a *desired* path. Rather than feeling anxiety every time you see your boss, you alter the established path so that you enter a meeting with curiosity rather than dread.

Instead of feeling frightened when you walk on a stage to give a speech, you can alter the path so that you embrace the opportunity to share with the crowd rather than worry about their reaction to you. And rather than feeling infuriated or threatened when you see a person who has upset you in the past, you can interact with them feeling stable and on solid ground.

Because your brain works from the inside out, you must start your training with the emotional brain. Later in the book, we'll talk about how to use your body and breath to help train your brain further. For now, let's focus on four powerful techniques to help you change your reactions: Noticing, Affect Labeling (also called Naming), Scratch the Record, and Meditation.

Technique One: Noticing

The perception → recognition → action process is highly adaptable, allowing you to adjust your actions in response to changing sensory information and goals.

Each day, set aside a few minutes to practice noticing without judgment. In a nonthreatening, noncritical environment, take a few minutes to slow the transition from perceiving and recognizing.

As you are riding in a vehicle (assuming you are not the driver) or walking, notice what you see. Practice as you watch the scenery. Notice without judgment. Look at the trees and observe their height (not "tall"). What color are the leaves, the flowers, the fence? Judgment includes thoughts such as "ugly, pretty, big, comfortable, awkward," etc. Adjectives are judgmental. Just notice without any judgment.

Notice the differences in the table below between a judgment and noticing:

JUDGMENT		NOTICING
Oh what a beautiful field! -or- My allergies are going to hate this!		There are white flowers, which I believe are called daisies. There are purple flowers. The stems and grass are green. The sky is blue and has four clouds in it. The flowers take up about half of the space I can see.
Oh my! Get that rabbit out of my yard! -or- What a cute little bunny.		One brown rabbit with its eyes open is sitting in the grass with white flowers.
Ooh. That does *not* look comfortable at all. -or- Now that is a very contemporary-looking sofa. It would look good in my house.		The green sofa has three cushions on it. The four legs are made of wood. The arms of the sofa curve outwards.

BRAIN   51

At the end of the two weeks, Matt was astounded at the difference in how he approached situations. He realized he was habitually judgmental—more than he'd thought. He might see a person and think, "Ugh, they are dressed like a slob," or "They sure talk a lot." These seemingly benign judgments were constant and often overshadowed his simple awareness.

What I found most impactful from our coaching was the Noticing exercise: Focusing, being in the moment, and noticing what is happening without judgment has helped me to become naturally more aware. Not just when I'm doing the exercise. I recognize the environment, objects, and people for what they are (facts), not solely as my reactive judgments, which previously hindered my effectiveness.

At the time of our coaching, Matt was at the director level in his company. Years later he is president of a large consulting company and is still practicing Noticing, employing appropriately Noticing and Judging.

Abandoning judgment altogether would be both impractical and unwise. Judgment draws upon our accumulated life experiences and plays a crucial role in helping us distinguish between potential dangers and pleasures. However, deeply ingrained habits of quick, reflexive judgment can mean losing the capacity for simple observation and discernment. By intentionally slowing down and cultivating the ability to rewire your automatic responses in the perception → recognition → action chain, you can effectively expand judgment by emphasizing recent experiences while incorporating your past. You can also reduce the frequency of unhelpful judgments, both toward others and yourself.

Technique Two: Naming

As discussed, the limbic system (emotional brain) determines the first emotional response to an event and quickly sends a message to your frontal cortex (thinking brain). Your thinking brain then drives your behavior. Redirecting behavior can be done by interrupting that split second of transmission between the emotional and the thinking brains. With time and repeated practice, the response level in your limbic system is reconditioned so that an event (meeting with your boss, important meeting with a client, public speaking, etc.) no longer elicits the "danger" signal.

TIP: "Naming" can be an effective emotion regulator even if it is unintentional. It is an effective strategy for both short-term and long-term regulation of our emotions.

Research conducted by Matthew D. Lieberman, PhD, neuroscience lab director at UCLA, suggests that using words, known as "affect labeling," can create a braking system in the brain.* Consciously choosing an emotion word, such as "anger, fear, sadness, etc." in the moment can have a regulating effect on the emotional experience. In Lieberman's studies, participants were shown emotionally suggestive images (e.g., snake, hospital scene, etc.) and asked to report their distress level. When participants

---

* Matthew D. Lieberman et al., "Putting Feelings into Words: Affect Labeling Disrupts Amygdala Activity to Affective Stimuli," *Psychological Science* 18 (2007): 421–428.

labeled their emotional state precisely when they were experiencing the emotion, they reported feeling less distress than if they simply observed the images.

In another study, subjects with arachnophobia (fear of spiders) spent time with a caged tarantula. Members in one group were asked to label their negative emotions, while a different group engaged in strategies such as distraction or reappraisal. Another group engaged no strategies. Researchers measured stress and physiological reaction by the subjects' skin-conductance response, indicating psychological or physiological arousal. The more the participants were able to label their emotions as they confronted the event, the more significant decrease their skin conductance response a week later. Not only was their skin conductance response decreased, but they were also able to move closer to the tarantula.

Other fMRI studies have shown that using affect labeling—or naming the emotion—physiologically altered brain activity. When subjects used affect labeling, a portion of the prefrontal cortex (thinking brain) associated with cognitive control and emotion regulation *increased* activity. At the same time, amygdala (emotional brain) activity in the region associated with fear and anxiety showed *reduced* activity when labeling or naming the emotion.

Affect labeling is believed to be helpful when it comes to any emotion you might consider "negative," such as vulnerability, shame, regret, anger, or fear.

Learning to immediately name the emotion you feel is a simple (but not easy) tip for overriding a fight, flight, or freeze impulse. By noticing and quickly naming the emotion, energy is more quickly redirected to your cortex rather than instinctively reacting to the amygdala's often faulty interpretation. It takes a lot of practice and a willingness to be mindful.

First, notice you're having an emotional reaction—perhaps the beginning of an amygdala hijack—then you quickly choose an emotion word and say it internally.

Your boss critiques your work. Internally label it: "insecure."

You prepare to go on stage for a speech. Internally name it: "scared."

You are having a challenging conversation with a client. Name it: "uncertainty."

TIP: By using "naming," over time the external stimuli—the ex, the boss, etc.—simply no longer produces an "unsafe" message from the amygdala, thus eliminating the emotional reaction from you.

The prefrontal cortex is engaged as you name each emotion, which allows you to *think* and *respond* rather than simply *feel* and *react*. Studies show that the continued naming of an event decreases the effects of that stimulus to mitigate the original interpretation. Over time, the amygdala no longer is triggered by the "unsafe" event—the ex, the boss, the erratic driver—thus subduing your instinctive emotional reaction.

Henry, the executive who instinctively reacted with overwhelming anxiety when encountering a former boss, had a default neural network of performing well. Throughout the years, he'd developed a strong identity as the "golden boy" and racked up a lifetime of successes. When his boss harshly and publicly berated him, the instinctive reaction from his limbic system was "unsafe." The event threatened his job, his position, his identity, and his security. That perceived threat from the boss firmly etched a neural pathway.

As a result of our coaching, Henry named his emotion "fear" when he felt the "unsafe" emotion, whether elicited by a conversation, a memo, or even a mention of the former boss's name. About five months after he began using the affective labeling technique, Henry came into our coaching session very excited:

"Margo, you won't believe what happened! After my speaking event, I was socializing with several colleagues, and everything was going great. The speech was a success; it was pleasant and invigorating to socialize with my colleagues. That evening when I got home, it hit me—Former Boss was there, socializing afterward—and I had no negative reaction. It didn't even register that 'he,' the source of such angst for so long, was even anyone other than a former colleague. I never imagined that would be possible!"

Naming emotions is an effective strategy for short-term and long-term regulation. The brain responds differently to a simple emotion word—disgust, fear, etc.—than when you have a lengthy internal monologue about your frustrations. For example, do not exclaim, "They make me so *angry* when they do that!" That becomes a directive and will activate other parts of your brain. The powerful effect of simply naming the emotion won't be realized.

Affect labeling, or naming, can have many positive effects, including improved emotional regulation, increased self-awareness, and reduced stress.

Important note: Because the one-word technique of naming an emotion *decreases* emotional response, it should be used only with emotions you want to minimize. If you want to *increase* emotional response to positive events, consciously noticing them while simply experiencing them can help rewire the brain for happiness. Consciously notice the joy, the warmth, the contentment in a given experience. Fully experience and acknowledge these positive feelings in the moment. Do not label, analyze, or rationalize the positive event. Simply bask in the positivity. Remember, affect labeling (or naming) *decreases* emotional impact; noticing *increases* the emotional impact.

For bilingual individuals, the language you use to label your emotions matters. Affect labeling in a nonnative language won't reduce amygdala activation or downregulate negative emotions. Label in your native language.

Technique Three: Scratch the Record

Karl, director at an engineering company, described himself as focused and driven. Despite hard work, multiple accomplishments, and a long tenure, he continually missed attaining a higher position. Troubled by his lack of professional progress, he began executive coaching to help him determine what he could be doing differently. When we began working together, he was going through a difficult time with a team he managed. When they didn't perform to his standards, he would withdraw the assignment and try to accomplish it himself. Rather than engaging with the team members to get input, he would issue directives. The team was underperforming, disengaged, and turnover was high. With increased awareness through coaching, he realized he wanted to repair the relationships rather than continue keeping his colleagues at a distance and inwardly criticizing them. Our coaching included team-building and communication techniques

BRAIN **57**

and skills, but Karl reported little shift in his behavior or reaction to the team.

The coaching engagement included a 360-assessment where Karl was assessed by his boss, his boss's boss, direct reports, and peers, in addition to completing a self-assessment. Because feedback was anonymous, there was a high probability of the assessors being honest in their feedback. Karl's assessment showed a high response rate in the "Distant" dimension, which indicates a tendency to establish a sense of personal worth and security through withdrawal, being superior, and remaining aloof, emotionally distant, and above it all.

After being passed over for yet another position that he felt qualified for and expected to get, we discussed his reaction—to "get safe" through withdrawal, retreat, and blaming others. Karl began to realize his immediate safety reaction was no longer supporting or protecting him and, in fact, stymied his growth.

For a coach, the source of his conditioning was irrelevant, but for Karl, understanding why "distance" meant safety and stability mattered.

Karl grew up with an alcoholic parent. He never knew if the funny drunk or the mean drunk would show up at home. He found "safety" by removing himself from his parent's presence. If the parent's car approached the house, he would turn off the light and be silent. After the parent went to bed, Karl would turn on the light and study. Karl's neural pathways were formed to create a survival mechanism—distance increased safety.

Karl's neural pathways continued to follow the path of least resistance as an adult: work hard, do the right thing, and, when he felt threatened, remain distant. His belief that he must please others is an example of the results of unconscious learning.

1. AWARENESS: Become aware of the specific pattern or behavior you want to change. Identify the thoughts, emotions, or actions that are not serving you or are hindering your progress.

2. RECOGNITION: As you notice the thought, emotion, or action occurring, simply notice that it is in the process of occurring.

3. INTERRUPTION: Consciously interrupt the pattern when it starts to emerge. Do not judge yourself; simply create a physical or mental interruption to disrupt the automatic response. It may be something as simple as taking a deep breath, pausing for a moment, or physically moving your body.

4. REPLACE WITH A NEW RESPONSE: After interrupting the pattern, intentionally replace it with a new response that aligns with your desired outcome.

Imagine his neural pathways as the grooves in a vinyl record, and the needle follows the established groove to play the programmed music. That's what was going on for Karl. Scratching the record creates a repetitive and jarring sound by manipulating the vinyl record. Tony Robbins, an internationally known motivational guru, refers to "scratching the record" as a metaphor to describe the process of disrupting or changing deeply ingrained patterns of thinking, feeling, or behaving that are no longer serving us.

How to make the scratch? First, notice when your brain's neurons start the negative or unhealthy thought process and consciously stop the "automatic playing." Noticing it makes a slight scratch in the record. The more you consciously notice the thought or emotion, the more the record will be scratched, lessening the path of least resistance.

I suggested that Karl begin by simply noticing when he withdrew from others, without judgment and without trying to change. Karl spent two weeks noticing when his distance surfaced and was surprised to see its appearance in all aspects of his life: at work, in social interactions, and with family relations. When things didn't go right (as he defined it), if people didn't agree with him, when people didn't follow the protocol or rules, Karl would write them off and withdraw.

After two weeks of simply noticing, I suggested Karl begin consciously replacing the withdrawal with taking a deep breath and saying, "Learning." Over the months that followed, Karl gradually noticed his "Withdraw!" response diminishing. A year later, he was happy to report the tendency surfaced only occasionally. He was able to recognize the reaction, and it no longer controlled him. Karl happily reached out to tell me he was able to lead more successfully, with greater ease and more positive impact, and had been recently promoted to senior vice president in his company.

Changing neural pathways takes conscious effort and time. It requires consistent practice and patience. By intentionally "scratching the record" of old patterns and replacing them with empowering responses, you can create positive changes in your life and align your thinking and behaviors with your goals and aspirations.

Technique Four: Meditation

Meditation is an ancient practice that, thanks to extensive study by modern science, has provided empirical evidence that it can change the brain.

If your immediate reaction to that sentence was, "I can't meditate! My brain won't stop thinking" or "I've tried it, and I wasn't good at it" (or "It didn't make a difference"), you're not alone. The reaction is common among clients when I talk about meditation. But this simple practice is merely a way to quieten the thinking brain and let the emotional brain rest for a while. It's as simple (but not easy!) as getting quiet, then still, and then noticing.

Imagine walking into a room with twenty-five TVs blaring, each on a different station. Throw in a few crying babies, yelling adults, and a temperature either too hot or too cold. Sensory overload!

Too often, this metaphoric overload is the daily diet of the thinking brain. You go, go, *go, go, go*, believing you can power through and make sense of everything happening around you.

Now imagine just stepping outside of that room into a quiet hallway. Take a deep breath. Then take another. Don't try to fix the room you just left; stay in the hall. Just be quiet, for a few minutes, in that space.

Meditation can be as simple as that—a few moments outside that crazy room. With consistent meditation, you will notice the activity without letting the activity control you.

BRAIN 61

No need to "turn off" the brain, which is neither possible nor desirable. The frontal lobe of our brain is designed to think. We wouldn't want the frontal lobe to stop doing its job any more than we would want the parietal lobe to stop sensing touch, or the occipital lobe to stop processing information from the eyes. But that doesn't mean it's not worth training the thinking brain to settle down and allowing the emotional brain to exercise calming effects.

Just as the thinking brain does more than think (it processes touch, input from the eyes, language, etc.), the emotional brain processes emotions, memories, and motivation, and more. Imagine that meditation makes the thinking brain calmer and the emotional brain more restful. Envision the thinking brain settling down like a tired body at the end of the day, becoming less active. Picture the emotional brain receiving a cool, soothing cover of calm. And notice your breath.

Jim Larsen, a senior instructor at the Art of Living Foundation, has been meditating daily since age nineteen. He has led personal development workshops internationally for more than forty years and has this to say: "Forcing yourself into a meditative state is like forcing yourself to sleep. You can't force yourself. Instead, you set the right conditions and wait for it to happen."

Many meditation practices exist, each with unique techniques and approaches—mindfulness meditation, transcendental meditation, Vipassana meditation, Zen meditation, and others. Regardless of the type, science has affirmed many benefits such as lowering stress, reducing anxiety, enhancing mental health, improving sleep, and more.

Studies using fMRI show that during meditation, the amygdala decreases activity. At the same time, the hippocampus, involved in memory and learning, lights up. Some studies suggest that continued meditation can increase gray matter, which has been linked to improved cognitive function.

The US National Institute of Health (NIH) has produced numerous reports on the benefits of meditation. One NIH report on a research study involved more than twelve thousand people with diagnosed psychiatric disorders, including anxiety and depression. It found that mindfulness-based meditation worked as well as evidence-based therapies (e.g., cognitive-based therapy, interpersonal therapy, psychodynamic therapy, etc.) to reduce symptoms. Another NIH report, with close to seventeen hundred participants, found that mindfulness meditation improved sleep quality more than education-based treatments.[*]

With fMRI, researchers can show that experienced meditators have less activation in the amygdala than novices when presented with disturbing visual stimuli and emotional sounds.[†] In addition to reducing the frequency and impact of amygdala hijacks, meditation can also increase activity in the insula, a part of the limbic system that contributes to emotional regulation and empathy. Other overall positive impacts of meditation on thinking include:

---

[*] NCCIH, "Meditation and Mindfulness: What You Need to Know," National Center for Complementary and Integrative Health, https://www.nccih.nih.gov/health/meditation-and-mindfulness-what-you-need-to-know.

[†] Richard J. Davidson and Antoine Lutz, "Buddha's Brain: Neuroplasticity and Meditation," *IEEE Signal Process Mag.* 25, no. 1 (January 1, 2008):174–176. doi: 10.1109/msp.2008.4431873. PMID: 20871742; PMCID: PMC2944261.

- Increased activity in the prefrontal cortex, which can lead to improved cognitive function and emotional regulation.
- Reduced activity in the default node network, which is active during passive moments. Reducing activity in the default node network makes you more relaxed during these passive moments, and the mind is less likely to wander into stressful territory.

One of my coaching clients, David, was highly skeptical of reaping the rewards of meditation. A colonel in the US military with global responsibilities, David had spent years struggling to overcome the effects of growing up in a highly dysfunctional environment. He had decided that emotional detachment was the key to success. His belief that he must resort to distance is another example of the results of unconscious learning.

Early in our coaching sessions, he articulated a great understanding of psychology, philosophy, and spirituality. He even knew psychology diagnosis codes and language, courtesy of longtime therapy. He knew his past negatively influenced his value as a leader and partner, and he was aware that certain types of people "set him off." He had self-awareness about the need to change and had intellectually studied methods to help him make the desired changes. Along the way, he had decided "finding enlightenment" was the answer and began working diligently toward it, including dating a yoga teacher for a while.

Unfortunately, although he was educated, well-informed, and was familiar with the emotional and thinking brains, he wasn't seeing the positive changes in himself he desired.

"I see these characters [people], and my amygdala just gets

hijacked!" he exclaimed to me, demonstrating his intellectual understanding of the different parts of the brain.

"What has been your experience with meditation?" I asked.

"Oh, I tried that—removing myself and looking at things objectively. All the meditation books talk about removing yourself from the world and escaping to some ashram to become enlightened."

There was such passion and desire in his voice, wanting to find "it." This single conversation with David encapsulates many misconceptions people hold about meditation, what it is, and the benefits you can experience.

"Enlightenment" is not the purpose or goal of meditation. Meditation does not require escaping from your daily world to practice and reap its benefits. It doesn't require sitting in lotus pose or chanting, "Om." A meditation practice requires only a bit of time, willingness, and commitment.

I would describe myself as type-A-plus when I first attempted meditation during a highly stressful time in my life. Among other things, I had ended a second marriage due to domestic abuse. I was desperate to find peace and willing to try almost anything. Following my pattern of research, I started searching for the "right book." I discovered that some meditation traditions counsel meditating twice a day, thirty minutes at a time. No way could I find that kind of time!

Instead, I started with five minutes.

I sat on my bedroom floor, leaning against the wall, and set my timer for five minutes. I forced myself to sit still for five minutes while silently narrating the words, "Inhale, exhale. Inhale. Exhale." When thoughts intruded, I imagined placing the thought on a shelf to be revisited later. Over time, my meditation practice became less forced and lasted longer. With persistence, I became a daily meditator.

I suggested that David start like that—five minutes a day. Being an overachiever, he started with ten minutes a day, focusing on his breath, noticing the inhales and exhales, and avoiding effort or judgment. Over the remaining months of our working together, he established a daily meditation practice. At our closing session, he talked about feelings and events without the expressions of disdain or judgment he often had used when we began working together. He was no longer reciting passages from books and manuals.

"To meet the challenges, I had to evolve," he said. "I am evolving."

Although he didn't attain the promotion to general he had hoped for, he learned how to embrace, rather than fight, his emotional brain and became a more effective, inspiring, and peaceful leader. He came to accept and embrace the leadership positions and opportunities that he was given.

Listening to guided relaxation reduces stress and should not be dismissed. But keep in mind that meditation is different from relaxation. Listening to guided imagery—imagining walking on the beach, a beautiful vision in the woods, or gleeful mental explorations—can be soothing and help you feel better. But that practice activates the thinking brain. Listening engages the temporal lobe, imagery engages the occipital lobe, and interpreting the words engages the frontal lobes.

Retraining the brain is best accomplished through meditation because rather than redirecting thoughts to images or mental activity, it quiets the thinking brain.

To set the conditions right, find a quiet place to sit comfortably without interruption. Sitting on the floor and leaning against a wall or sitting in a straight-backed chair with your feet touching the floor is fine. A timer can be helpful.

Soften your gaze toward the floor so that you are less inclined to be distracted by visual cues. Or, if you are comfortable with closing your eyes, do that.

Without judgment, notice your breathing, breathing only through your nose.

TIP: Simple start to meditation

1. Find a quiet place where you will not be interrupted.
2. Sit comfortably.
3. Set a timer for how long you'd like to meditate. Start with five minutes if that's what you feel most comfortable.
4. Soften your gaze toward the floor, or if you are comfortable, close your eyes.
5. Inhale through your nose, noticing your breathing.
6. Exhale through your nose, noticing your breathing.
7. If it helps you focus, find a word for your inhale and your exhale. You might simply say, "Inhale," "Exhale," or "I" on the inhale, and "Am" on the exhale.
8. As thoughts enter your mind—and they will—notice them and return to being aware of your breath.
9. Continue inhale. Exhale.
10. When the timer goes off, turn off the timer and sit quietly for a moment as you open your eyes and reenter the physical space.

Observe your inhalation. Observe your exhalation. Just notice. Inhale. Exhale. If it helps you to better focus, find a word for your inhale and your exhale. You might simply say, "Inhale," "Exhale," or "I" on the inhale, and "Am" on the exhale.

As thoughts enter your mind—and they will—notice them and return to being aware of your breath. Inhale. Exhale.

Start with five minutes and work your way up to more time. Like any training—preparing for a marathon, practicing a musical instrument, studying for a degree—regular, repeated practice will reap greater rewards.

Now go back to one of the earlier scenarios—the boss, your annoying colleague, or the car cutting you off. The event occurs, and the stimulus enters your emotional brain. With reduced activity in the amygdala and in a less frazzled state, the emotional brain can interpret the stimuli and send it more calmly (or at least less frazzled) to your thinking brain for action.

Healthy eating and exercise habits improve your overall health; however, they do not prevent you from all health maladies. The fittest athletes and the most diligent healthy eaters still get sick occasionally, but their bodies are at a better starting point for rebounding to health. Likewise, meditation is not a cure-all for all mental or emotional stress. It simply helps you be better equipped to manage—and enjoy—life.

While meditation and yoga have been proven to improve physical, mental, and emotional health, we are all humans who encounter stress and emotional challenges. Do not be hard on yourself if you still experience stress or anxiety after regularly practicing meditation. Although meditation can and does calm the limbic system, it does not remove all of life's stressors. It simply helps us better cope with our challenges.

If you want to learn more about meditation, find a yoga studio or meditation center close to you, or search the internet for books and apps that help guide you through meditation. If you try one method for meditation and it doesn't fit right for you, try another. I use a yoga Nidra recording when I find myself having trouble sleeping. When I recommended it to my adult daughter, she said, "How can you listen to that? I find his voice annoying." So find the meditation practice that works for you.

Important note regarding meditation: Meditation and mindfulness are not intended to replace conventional care or as a reason to postpone seeing a health-care provider about a mental health or medical problem.

Summary

The vast wonder and potential of the awe-inspiring brain extends far beyond what has been touched upon here. Unraveling the complexities within your skull grants you the ability to embrace and leverage this potential, steering you away from being held captive by default reactions. Understanding the inner workings of this magnificent organ empowers you to harness its power effectively rather than being at the mercy of default reactions. Embracing the emotional brain's significance can profoundly influence the capabilities of the thinking brain. By integrating and exercising your emotional intelligence, you can unlock the keys to personal and professional success, fostering a sense of security and adaptability.

Proactively engaging with neuroplasticity enables you to rewire learned behaviors, fostering healthier responses to life's challenges. Discerning between noticing and judging can alter how you interpret others and yourself. And with conscious choice, training techniques like naming, scratching the record, and meditation offer opportunities to shape a brighter future.

In the next section, Body, we'll venture into the fascinating interplay between the autonomic nervous system and the brain, delving into how they jointly shape your emotional state and overall health and well-being. By shedding light on these intricate connections, you can deepen your understanding of yourself, open doors to greater self-awareness and personal growth, and foster resilience and adaptability in the face of life's challenges.

CHAPTER 3

BODY

Your body provides you with infinite information—if you're willing to pay attention to its signals. But in modern life's fast and frenetic drumbeat, too often, the messages your body sends can go unnoticed, get ignored, or are dismissed.

When you think of your body, how do you measure its health? What is its value to you? Would your assessment revolve around metrics such as weight, blood pressure, sugar levels, and body mass index? Might it include measuring how fast you can run, your endurance level, how much weight you can bench-press, or how flexible you are?

A question worth considering is how your body reinforces your role as a leader and, on the flip side, how it might inadvertently strip you of potency. A lack of awareness and understanding could mean you're overlooking the profound potential of what your body does (and can do) for you, extending far beyond the tangible measures that meet the eye.

Two leaders I worked with, Sam and Pat, for years had

overlooked signals their bodies sent to them, which eventually led to significant negative effects on their leadership capabilities, their minds, and their relationships.

Sam was a regional director of a multinational corporation, which encompassed significant global responsibilities. With nearly three decades of corporate expertise, he was widely recognized and deeply respected within the information technology community. Some even referred to him as a legend.

When we began working together, Sam was experiencing significant professional and personal turmoil. He had an extraordinary reputation as a turnaround agent, but after six months in a new position, he found himself constantly questioning his knowledge, understanding, and value as a leader. Sam's thirty-year marriage also was foundering, and he questioned whether he and his spouse would manage to "ride off into the sunset together."

The person who showed up for our coaching sessions did not resemble the person others perceived him to be—or the person he knew himself to be. Sam wasn't sleeping when he was supposed to—at night. He was sleeping when he wasn't supposed to—all weekend. He struggled with clarity and decision-making and became increasingly irritable.

Sam was very attuned to his physical metrics (weight, cholesterol, blood sugar, blood pressure). He described to me in detail how he had gained seven pounds and what he was doing to lose the unwanted weight. But he wasn't aware of how his daily presence was affected by the autonomic nervous system, which is the control center for sleep, mental clarity, mood, and pain perception.

Another client, Pat, CEO of a $250 million consulting company, was referred to me by one of her colleagues. Pat's company was fighting a legal assault—or ambush, as Pat described it—from a former partner. She also saw her executive team as underperforming. Her biggest problem, as she described it, was exhaustion. "How do I turn off my brain?" she asked me in one of our sessions.

Both leaders were considered successful. And neither recognized the high costs their success was having on their health, peace of mind, and relationships. They needed strategies for achieving mindful success.

Our work together included helping both Sam and Pat recognize that they couldn't "think" their way out of their dilemmas. To help them deal more effectively with their challenges, we had to delve into how the body functions and the intricacies of the nervous system influence their behaviors, mental acuity, emotional health, and relationships.

In my own life, I received a profound and painful lesson about how the body works in my thirtieth year. A head-on collision with a drunk driver left me with multiple broken vertebrae and multiple other serious injuries. One descriptive doctor said the accident had shredded every muscle, tendon, and ligament from my head to my butt.

Recovery required me to lie flat for almost four months. When I returned home, I had to kneel and rest my body on my legs to bathe. Getting to the kitchen for food meant crawling down a short hall, but because I was so weak, I had to stop halfway and lay on the floor to rest. I could not even read because of recurring, severe vertigo.

Western medicine, with its x-rays, MRIs, and surgery, helped me recover physically, but in the process, I became addicted to muscle relaxers and pain pills. Months after the accident, and still barely able to walk, I drove to the pharmacist with a paper bag full of prescription medicine. "What are all of these?" I asked the pharmacist.

Her face looked troubled. "Are you taking *all* of these?"

"I'm prescribed all of them, but I don't think I should take them all."

With the help of that excellent pharmacist, I learned how the different medications affected my body. For example, muscle relaxers depress the central nervous system by slowing or interfering with nerve transmissions. While they relaxed my muscles, they also affected vital body functions, such as breathing. Percocet and other pain medicines reduced back pain but included side effects of dizziness, sleepiness, and confusion.

With time and determination, I weaned myself off the medication. It was three years before I stopped wishing I had died in the accident, but ever so slowly, I began to regain my health and stamina.

Before the accident, I had taken pride in my ability to withstand physical discomfort or pain, viewing my capacity to disregard those sensations as strength and resilience. At one pre-accident doctor appointment, she asked about the location of my stomach discomfort. I proudly claimed, "I don't know. I don't pay attention to that." For most of my professional career, I'd soldier on to work, even if I was unwell, seeing that as dedication and a badge of honor.

But I learned the hard way that ignoring what my body was telling me was dangerous. If—as history had taught me—I could improve myself through understanding the brain, what might I gain by learning more about the body's role in my continued self-improvement?

A terrible accident jolted me into realizing the urgency of tuning into my body's signals, but hopefully, most people can respond to more subtle signals. Unfortunately, these signals are easily overlooked or explained away.

In addition to sleepless nights and lack of clear thinking, leaders I work with often talk about tension in their shoulders or tightness in their backs or hips. They suffer from headaches or other physical pains. Like I used to do, they muscle through the sensations or focus on eliminating immediate discomfort. They rarely pause to decipher the origins of these signals or unravel the potentially profound messages and warning signals their bodies may be conveying. Too often, they accept physical and mental pain as the price of being successful.

The body is vast, extending beyond the tangible skin, bones, muscles, tendons, ligaments, and organs that can be physically sensed and measured. Inside resides a remarkable network of more than seven trillion nerves, constituting your body's intricate nervous system. These nerves are like the body's electrical wiring, transmitting signals between your brain, spinal cord, and throughout your body. Nerves also control body functions such as digesting food and maintaining heart rate. Problems such as weakness, numbness, and pain are often the first ways the nervous system gets your serious attention.

Understanding and appreciating the complexities of the nervous system is critical for cultivating robust well-being and establishing a conducive state to support your leadership journey. Regrettably, many individuals embrace the philosophy of "out of sight, out of mind." If nerves remain unseen and untouched, their power and potential are often ignored, a profound wellspring of capability overlooked due to its unseen nature.

My intention is to illuminate the significance of cultivating awareness and grace within your body while delving into the complexities of your nervous system, which are usually difficult to measure. This facet, often overlooked by conventional Western medicine, houses a priceless instrument that holds the potential to enhance a leader's performance and efficacy significantly.

Your Nervous Systems

I once led a workshop for a core project team at the US Department of Transportation. The team was responsible for a significant, massive project that would affect travel and transportation across the United States and was composed of highly qualified leaders in engineering, software development and integration, communications, acquisition, and risk management. The senior program manager was responsible for the overall project, which was the equivalent of trying to turn a massive ship with more moving parts than most people can imagine within the federal government. Many important eyes were looking out for this project's success.

The team had done an impressive job of selecting the right members, clearly identifying roles, responsibilities, and authority, and attending to the importance of the team performing as a *team*, not just as a group of highly qualified individuals assigned to work together. The ten-member core planning team also invested in ensuring the "team spirit" extended to the more than fifty members. The project was going to be multiyear, and the leader was aware of a risk—could team members remain in good health to see it across the finish line?

They also recognized the effect the intense work was having on their bodies, including tight shoulders, back pain, and waking in the middle of the night. Because they knew I taught yoga, they invited me to share stretching exercises to relieve workplace stress. They were surprised when I started explaining the role of their nervous system, specifically their central and peripheral nervous systems, and how the movements I was teaching them also affected their blood pressure, pain perception, mood, and mental clarity.

The team members enjoyed the workshop, often laughing at the poses or making fun of the breathing techniques; however, I was curious what the long-term impact was on them as individuals and as a team. Following up with them six months later, I found that most, although not all, of the participants had adopted some of the practices introduced, and all who had adopted the practices reported favorable outcomes. The senior program manager, who was perhaps the most stressed of the team, said she began practicing the poses and breathing techniques to help her feel centered, strong, and confident. She also adapted one of the breathing techniques, introduced in the next section, before going into the office in the morning and after leaving the office in the afternoon, sitting in her car for just a couple extra minutes to practice. She was skeptical at first but found over time that her emotional reactions were more balanced, and she was able to process the day's events more evenly. She also reported recognizing an immediate calming effect and became aware of her posture, then making adjustments when she found herself in a particularly challenging meeting. The senior program manager also began incorporating a few minutes of mindfulness into her team meetings, which she reported had resulted in a ripple effect of an overall healthier and more balanced team, producing even better results.

Another team member, a competitive golfer, was amazed at the impact the body positions and the breathwork had on her game, improving it significantly. And those members who had been practicing yoga before the workshop recognized how they could improve their work interactions and results by integrating the physical postures and breathing into their everyday work world.

While the brain is considered the master communicator in higher-level cognitive functions and decision-making, the human nervous system is an intricate network responsible for transmitting signals and facilitating communication between different body parts. It's like a sophisticated information highway relaying messages at lightning speed. You might think of your nervous system as a symphony conductor, coordinating every movement, sensation, and thought. It directs your conscious actions and manages various unconscious functions, such as breathing, digestion, and heartbeat. This interconnected marvel constantly processes, adapts, and responds to the ever-changing environment, making it an indispensable player in your physical and mental well-being.

Understanding this complex system's nuances provides insights into how you perceive, react, and navigate the world. When you are armed with this knowledge, you possess a unique capacity to adapt and regulate not only your actions but also how you lead and influence others in business. Integrating this knowledge into your daily activities offers a strategic advantage, empowering you to navigate challenges, make informed decisions, and foster a productive, harmonious professional environment.

In essence, it's an invaluable tool for enhancing your leadership and organizational effectiveness.

This system comprises two primary divisions: **the Central Nervous System (CNS)**, which is the command center consisting of the brain and spinal cord, and the **Peripheral Nervous System (PNS)**, which includes the nerves outside the brain and spinal cord and is a vast web of nerves extending throughout the body.

The Peripheral Nervous System is further divided into two pivotal facets, the **somatic nervous system** and the **autonomic nervous system,** which serve as conduits for relaying crucial information between the central nervous system—your brain and spinal cord—and the complex web of your body.

The **somatic nervous system** primarily governs voluntary movements and conscious sensory perceptions. It coordinates muscle contractions and enables people to interact with the external environment. When you raise your hand or kick a ball, the somatic nervous system orchestrates these intentional actions. It also facilitates awareness of sensory experiences such as touch, temperature, pain, and proprioception (the sense of the body's position in space).

In contrast, the **autonomic nervous system** controls automatic physiological functions that sustain life, usually without conscious awareness. This system is further subdivided into two branches: the **sympathetic** and **parasympathetic** nervous systems.

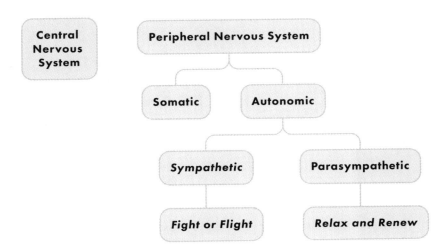

Like others, I always assumed that while voluntary muscle movements of our legs, arms, torso, etc., could be strengthened through exercise and repetitive practice and creating muscle memory, humans were powerless over our autonomic nervous system. Science has proven my previous assumption erroneous.

The Autonomic Nervous System (ANS)

Through yoga teacher training and Yoga as Therapy classes, I began to understand the intricate workings of the autonomic nervous system (ANS). The body has a triad of interconnected mechanisms, each with its distinct purpose. Understanding their functions opened the door to a compelling realization: with dedication, practice, and the passage of time, you possess the potential to exert tangible influence over intricate systems that operate beneath the surface.

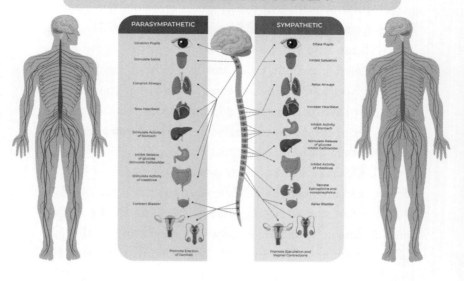

This knowledge opens a compelling avenue: the ability to steer the autonomic nervous system toward more favorable outcomes. By leveraging this understanding, you can actively shape and guide these invisible forces in ways that align with your leadership goals and objectives, ultimately enhancing your executive management and decision-making prowess.

Using a computer analogy, the brain functions as the body's "central processing unit" (CPU). It processes sensory information, controls motor functions, regulates body functions, and facilitates cognitive processes such as thinking, memory, and decision-making. The ANS is a network of interconnected components and processes that work to regulate bodily functions.

Understanding the autonomic nervous system can help you achieve your leadership goals more mindfully, whether trying to get enough restful sleep to maintain clear thinking, staying calm in stressful situations, confidently speaking in public, or successfully responding to and collaborating with others. Managing the ANS can help you productively manage feelings of being overwhelmed or anxious. It can provide a sense of strength when doubting yourself. And when you get too full of yourself, you can use it to invoke patience and humility. Conversely, ignoring the impact of the ANS can and is likely to send you into a state of reactivity and diminished effectiveness.

A colleague, Alexander, recounted the story of Jim, an account leader for a prominent defense contractor in Washington, DC. Jim had started his day with enthusiasm. As he settled into his desk at 8:00 a.m., he received a text from a colleague informing him that the client had issued a "request for proposal" to other consulting firms. This unexpected news triggered a surge of anxiety and fear within Jim, and he felt himself begin to sweat. Why was the client seeking alternatives? Jim believed he had a solid rapport with the client, built on open communication. If they were dissatisfied, shouldn't they have conveyed their concerns directly?

Within minutes, Jim's anxiety escalated along with his heartbeat as he imagined his company losing the project, potentially jeopardizing his anticipated promotion and bonus. His stomach ached as he began questioning his worth as a consultant. By 8:15 a.m., feeling angry, he resolved to avoid the client and dedicated the morning to crafting a persuasive PowerPoint presentation to convince them of their consulting firm's superiority.

By 8:20 a.m., he felt nauseous. He began mentally preparing his resignation letter. To lose this account would be the end of his career.

What transpired here? Jim received information from a colleague, interpreted it as a threat, and unconsciously activated his sympathetic nervous system, triggering a fight-or-flight response. Had Jim possessed awareness of the sympathetic nervous system (fight-or-flight) and its counterpart, the parasympathetic nervous system (relax-and-renew), he could have employed simple techniques to recalibrate his body and mind. This would have enabled him to gather more information and respond calmly and effectively rather than succumbing to immediate stress and fear.

The autonomic nervous system contains the sympathetic nervous system and the parasympathetic nervous system. Nerves from the sympathetic nervous system (SNS) and parasympathetic nervous system (PNS) extend throughout your body, spanning from head to toe. These two systems are in a continuous dialogue with your brain, transmitting signals that assess whether you are in a state of safety or facing potential danger.

Sympathetic Nervous System

The sympathetic nervous system (SNS) mobilizes the body for action; it controls the fight-or-flight-or-freeze response. The term "fight or flight," used to describe an animal's instinctive response to threat, was first used in 1915 by Walter Bradford Cannon, MD, an American physiologist, professor, and chairman of Harvard Medical School's Department of Physiology. He described it as "a physiological reaction that occurs in response to a perceived harmful event, attack, or threat to survival."* This

---

* Walter B. Cannon, *Bodily Changes in Pain, Hunger, Fear and Rage: An Account of Recent Researches into the Function of Emotional Excitement* (New York: D. Appleton & Company, 1915).

response is beneficial if a speeding car is barreling toward you, or a wild animal is poised to attack. Unfortunately, the SNS is the same for a real threat (speeding car) or a perceived one (an unexpected email that your client has put out an RFP).

Not surprisingly, the SNS and the amygdala, addressed in the Brain section, are tightly interconnected. When the amygdala detects a threat or perceives a stressful situation, it activates the SNS's fight-or-flight response, which stimulates the release of stress hormones like adrenaline and noradrenaline, increases heart rate and blood pressure, dilates airways, and redirects blood flow to vital organs.

Likewise, the sympathetic nervous system can influence the amygdala's sensitivity to fear-inducing stimuli. Increased activity in the sympathetic nervous system can lead to heightened emotional reactions and increased vigilance in the amygdala. It's a two-way street—the SNS influences the amygdala, and the amygdala influences the SNS. Left unchecked, they can warp out of control, resulting in unhealthy reactions.

For example, the heart-pounding, stomach-tightening you feel as you deliver an important presentation is an indication that your sympathetic nervous system is in overdrive. When your throat is constricted and you struggle to breathe, it is the overactive SNS. When you are irritable, distracted, and fatigued, that's the sympathetic nervous system in high gear.

In today's world, with its fast-paced change, tight deadlines, demanding customers, and exasperating traffic, the fight-or-flight response produced by a hypervigilant amygdala and an overactive sympathetic nervous gets plenty of exercise and reinforcement.

Parasympathetic Nervous System

The parasympathetic nervous system (PNS) is often referred to as the regulator of the relax-and-renew response. It slows the heartbeat and dilates blood vessels thus improving blood flow and lowering blood pressure. After high stress or intense activity, it promotes rest, relaxation, and restoration by decreasing the heart rate, constricting the pupil of the eyes, increasing blood flow to digestive organs, and lowering blood pressure.

Because people are not typically aware of the vital role of the PNS, they don't consider the importance of exercising or strengthening it. Often, the only time the PNS gets "exercised" is during sleep. And unfortunately, as I begin the coaching process, restless, sleepless nights are oft-cited problems for many executives.

An integral part of the parasympathetic nervous system is the vagus nerve, which plays a major role in regulating parasympathetic functions. The vagus is the primary cranial nerve that carries parasympathetic signals from the brain to many organs in the body, including the heart, lungs, stomach, and intestines. This long nerve makes up 75 percent of the nerve tissue in your parasympathetic nervous system and is often described as the "wandering" nerve because of its extensive reach throughout the body.

Introducing the ANS and its effect on their minds and bodies was helpful for Sam and Pat, the coaching clients who were struggling with sleeplessness, lack of clarity, and irritability. They each wanted to understand the science behind it and were eager to try practical tools I recommended to improve their situations. After providing information about the autonomic nervous system, they could visualize what was happening in their bodies. They also began using breathing techniques (introduced in the next section) and became more aware of the messages their bodies were sending to their brains.

Sam has made steady progress in his mental clarity, sleep, mood, and confidence. While it requires a consistent, conscious practice of physical postures and breathwork, he says the rewards he sees are worth the work he invests.

Physical Awareness

How does understanding the nervous system of one's body help you become a better, more mindful leader? How does it support you to become mindfully successful rather than just exhausted by success? Just as the different parts of your brain work together seamlessly, so do the autonomic nervous system and your brain work together and influence each other.

Being a leader can be akin to running a marathon or competing in a triathlon. Who trains for competition by sitting around uttering affirmations? Instead, you prepare the body through a gradual buildup of strength and endurance by lengthening runs, cycling, and swimming. Leaders, akin to endurance athletes, navigate high-stress terrains frequently. Curiously, however, many prepare by trying to "talk" themselves into calmness or strategizing ways to wrest control. A repeated chorus of "Calm down!" becomes the refrain, as if the brain was going to be an obedient conductor responding to the mind's commands.

In exploring the brain's expanse, simple yet powerful tools were introduced—such as affect labeling and meditation—to soothe the turbulent currents of the limbic system. Of course, the brain, thoughts, and mind do not operate in isolation from the body. Rather, it's a synchronized battle formation in which body and mind march in unison. A relentless exchange of messages unfurls in a dual direction—dispatches from the amygdala and limbic stronghold embark upon a journey to the body's frontier while the echoes of the body's stance reverberate back, fusing into an intricate combat strategy. The fragile equilibrium between body and brain is fortified and upheld within this choreographed combat, ensuring an unwavering alliance.

The table below depicts some of the impacts of the sympathetic and parasympathetic nervous systems on your physical bodily functions. By understanding the tools to affect the nervous systems, you can modulate functions such as heart rate, mood, and mental clarity.

SYMPATHETIC	BODY FUNCTION	PARASYMPATHETIC
Increased	Heart rate / blood pressure	Decreased
Fast, chest and shallow	Breathing	Slow, diaphragm and deep
Increased	Pain perception	Decreased
Light, fatigued	Sleep	Deep, restful
Depleted	Immune system	Optimized
Irritable, depressed	Mood	Moderated
Hypervigilant, distracted	Mental clarity	Clear, focused
Elevated	Blood sugar / weight gain	Controlled
Diminished	Balance	Enhanced

If the fight-or-flight response is consistently triggered and heightened by the sympathetic nervous system, what is likely to happen when someone says something you interpret as critical? You are unlikely to respond calmly with the thought, "Hmm . . . that is one perspective to consider." A more common reaction might be, "How dare they say that? They don't even know what they're talking about" (fight response), or "Are they saying I'm not doing my job? Maybe I should just find a new job" (flight response).

An amazingly powerful tool in your daily work is to use posture and physical poses to affect clear thinking and stabilize feelings. When you stand with your chest pushed out and your shoulders back, not only do your back and neck begin to hurt, but the nerves are also signaling, "Danger! Ready for battle!" When you sit hunched over a desk or steering wheel, your back and neck nerves signal, "Danger. Ready to retreat." In either position, your body is activating the sympathetic nervous system, which can possibly lead to irritability, distraction, and feeling hypervigilant and overly sensitive.

Learning to maintain your body in a neutral position takes awareness, practice, and time. When I work with clients, I am often reminded of the beginning students I taught in yoga— from the extremely buff, muscular athlete to the young, thin college student and the new parent. Everyone has perceptions of their bodies: I am strong. I am thin and flexible. I have stamina and can go forever! But when I asked them to place weight on all parts of the foot and then lift their toes, I often saw confusion, followed by frustration. In a forward bend, they would bend their knees and round their backs rather than use a block as support. And as I guided them to Mountain Pose, which is basically standing with alignment and strength, new students were often disinterested. The pose was too subtle for some, not active or dynamic. In bodies that were habitually misaligned, it felt unnatural. Typically, they were more eager to learn headstands, arm balances, or other "cool yoga tricks."

I watched inexperienced students strain themselves in challenging poses, holding their breath, and pushing too hard. As they struggled, I saw reactions of "Forget it; I can't do that pose," or forceful semblance of the pose and, "Whew, I did it!" Often, they would compare themselves to other students and judge themselves as inadequate.

These students' practice on the mat was a metaphor for how they approached life—and a reflection of how I often see busy executives: They are in a hurry. They force themselves to go beyond what is natural or needed. They're disembodied and unaware, and unwilling to accept help. In their urgent quest to "get there," wherever there is, they miss the simple nuances that help one move through their yoga practice—and life—with greater ease.

Physical Movement

A wide range of individuals and organizations from the healthcare, fitness, education, and public health sectors have collectively stressed the importance of physical exercise for maintaining good health and quality of life with guidelines like thirty daily minutes of activity, five thousand daily steps, combining strength and aerobic training, and proper stretching. Most, if not all, cultures acknowledge exercise's positive effects on muscles, the heart, and breathing.

Yet a deeper dive into exercise reveals a crucial impact on autonomic nervous systems: sympathetic (fight-or-flight) and parasympathetic (relaxation and renewal). High-intensity activities activate fight-or-flight, while yoga, tai chi, and qigong engage the parasympathetic system.

We're wired for an active sympathetic system, which is vital for survival responses. The parasympathetic system, vital for restoration, needs conscious attention. Irrespective of individual personality types, leadership styles, or aspirations, nurturing a healthy parasympathetic nervous system offers pivotal support in becoming a more effective, empowered, and serene leader.

Physical exercise prompts endorphin release, leading to temporary pain relief and mood enhancement. The endorphins bind to opioid receptors, reducing pain perception and boosting well-being. Exercise benefits the limbic system, regulating emotions and stress through neurotransmitters and hormone control. It aids neuroplasticity, brain adaptation. However, it's important to note that endorphin levels revert to their usual state after activities like vigorous exercise, laughter, specific foods, music, or sex, resulting in a transient sense of euphoria.

Intense environments benefit from vigorous exercise, releasing endorphins. Yet, the fight-or-flight system needs respite, and the parasympathetic system must be strengthened.

What to Do

If you cannot consciously command your sympathetic and parasympathetic nervous systems directly by thinking, what's the solution?

Science has shown there are ways to influence the ANS despite its automatic functioning. For example, consistent high stress, real or perceived, amps up the fight-or-flight response, as does intense exercise. Meditation, breathwork, and yoga, on the other hand, impact the relax-and-renew response.

Learning how specific body postures, poses, and movements affect the sympathetic and parasympathetic nervous systems can allow you to bolster the relaxation responses and manage fight-or-flight reactions.

Through the integration of meditation, physical posture, and breathwork, you have the capability to pacify the sympathetic (fight-or-flight) system while enhancing the parasympathetic (relax-and-renew) system. In the Breath section, I will delve into the influence of breathing on your nervous system. But for now, I will introduce physical postures capable of recalibrating the signals your body sends, promoting the activation of the relax-and-renew (parasympathetic) system and a calming effect on the fight-or-flight (sympathetic) system.

Mindful adjustments to your posture, coupled with targeted exercises and mindfulness practices, can effectively modulate your autonomic nervous system. This results in tempering the sympathetic system and activating the parasympathetic system. The outcome is a calm mood rather than irritably, more focused mental clarity, and an enhanced sense of balance and well-being. Such a state cultivates better decisions, attentive listening, and empathetic engagement with colleagues, collaborators, and clients.

There's a Pose for That

The extensive study of yoga practice—including poses (asanas), breathwork (pranayama), and meditation—provides validation for the anecdotal and historical narratives suggesting that yoga contributes to enhanced well-being, particularly through its association with the parasympathetic nervous system.

The *Journal of Family Medicine and Primary Care* reported in July 2022 that participants who regularly practiced yoga demonstrated diminished sympathetic (fight-or-flight) activity and improved parasympathetic (relax-and-renew) activity.[*] The *Journal of Clinical and Diagnostic Research* reported on a 2013 study showing that, for healthy young women, regular yoga practice increased parasympathetic activity, which positively benefited the autonomic functions and psychological well-being in both pre- and postphases of their menstrual cycles.[†] According to the *International Journal of Preventive Medicine*, mind-body exercises such as yoga suppressed sympathetic (fight-or-flight) activity, reduced stress and anxiety, and improved autonomic and higher neural center functioning.[‡] Some of the autonomic reactivity tests used in these studies included resting heart rate, response of heart rate to standing, response of heart rate to deep breathing, response of blood pressure to standing, and sustained handgrip.

Activities that stretch and strengthen muscles are beneficial for stress reduction and overall well-being. However, yoga

---

[*]   R. Shobana et al., "Effect of Long-Term Yoga Training on Autonomic Function among the Healthy Adults," *J Family Med Prim Care* 11, no. 7 (July 2022): 3471–3475. doi: 10.4103/jfmpc.jfmpc_199_21. Epub July 22, 2022. PMID: 36387716; PMCID: PMC9648241.

[†]   Sarita Kanojia et al., "Effect of Yoga on Autonomic Functions and Psychological Status during Both Phases of Menstrual Cycle in Young Healthy Females," *J Clin Diagn Res.* 7, no. 10 (2013): 2133–2139.

[‡]   P. Sengupta, "Health Impacts of Yoga and Pranayama: A State-of-the-Art Review," *Int J Prev Med.* 3, no. 7 (July 2012): 444–458. PMID: 22891145; PMCID: PMC3415184.

goes beyond the benefits of physical exercise by regulating your autonomic nervous system and favoring restful responses (parasympathetic) over fight-or-flight reactions (sympathetic). Yoga postures involve more than mere physical positioning; they entail intention, discipline, awareness of minor adjustments and breath, humility, and kindness, qualities that extend from the mat to daily life.

A wealth of resources is available for yoga poses, known as *asanas*, showing how each pose and its alignment can trigger diverse physiological responses—some soothing and others that enhance physical openness. A complete yoga asanas practice including sitting poses, standing poses, forward bends, backbends, twists, balance poses, and reclining poses, is believed to stimulate every portion of the vagus nerve, which induces the relax-and-renew reaction.

Even if you're not participating in a complete practice, you can get great benefit by drawing upon certain poses. The list below offers pose categories that yield specific benefits. These poses can be easily adapted to fit work environments, and the focus here is not to turn you into a yogi but to adopt physical postures that activate the parasympathetic nervous system for desired outcomes of feeling centered, calm, strong, or more patient.

With practice, these unfamiliar poses become natural, with consistent practice, the parasympathetic nervous system stays engaged, fostering serenity and heightened effectiveness.

WHEN YOU NEED HELP . . .	PRACTICE THESE POSTURES
Feeling Centered	Seated or Lying Poses
Feeling Strong	Standing or Warrior Poses
Speaking Up for What You Need	Chest Openers
Energizing	Chest Openers
Release of Emotions	Hip Opener
Cooling	Hip Opener
Humility	Forward Bends
Patience	Forward Bends
Cleansing (Emotional or Physical)	Twists
Relaxing / Letting Go	Restorative Poses

To Feel Centered

Feeling scattered? Pulled in too many directions? Or just a bit out of control? The centering poses and postures in this section can help you regain calm and balance and provide a state of inner equilibrium and emotional balance. Stress, anxiety, and external pressures might still exist, but a centered person is better equipped to navigate these challenges with composure and resilience. When you feel centered, you're likely to experience a sense of calm, stability, and harmony within yourself, regardless of external circumstances or pressures. This state of emotional equilibrium often leads to better decision-making, improved interpersonal relationships, and a more positive outlook on life.

Feeling centered is not a fixed state; it's a dynamic and ongoing process that requires continuous self-awareness and effort to maintain. Yoga poses such as seated easy pose (Sukhasana), and mountain pose (Tadasana) will help you feel grounded and centered. Both are easily adaptable for when you are in public. Assuming these postures can be useful, for example, right before a presentation or before a client meeting with key stakeholders.

Mountain Pose (Tadasana): Stand with feet together, weight evenly distributed between both feet. Think about gently grounding all four "corners" of the feet. Bring attention to your body, from your feet up: lift your kneecaps and engage your quadriceps (thigh) muscles. In your pelvic area, lengthen the tailbone toward the floor and pull your belly button up and back toward the spine. Broaden the collar bones, and relax the shoulders and shoulder blades. Turn your biceps and palms to face forward. Lengthen the neck and align it with your spine, even on all sides with your head balanced evenly over your body. Keep your body awareness as you inhale slowly and deeply, and exhale long and slow.

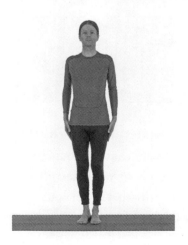

Seated easy pose (Sukhasana), traditionally entails sitting on the ground in a cross-legged position. At work, assuming a seated, cross-legged position in the floor at work might attract unwelcome attention, but an adaptation of the pose is still useful. Sit on the edge of the chair with glutes firmly on the seat, with sit bones and spine away from the back of the chair. Place your feet flat on the floor and rest your hands on your knees or on the arm rests of the chair. Sit straight with a long spine, belly button up and in toward your spine. As in Tadasana, align your neck so it feels long and even on all sides and balance your head evenly over your body. With awareness throughout your body, inhale slowly and deeply, and exhale long and slow.

Both of these postures induce a neutral physical state. You're neither pushing out your chest nor hunching over. Keeping your body in relaxed alignment while breathing slowly and deeply activates the parasympathetic nervous system and sends the message to your limbic system that you are safe.

To Feel Strong or Confident

Do you need a boost to carry you successfully through those meetings or projects? Standing poses such as Warrior (Virabhadrasana) I, II, and III, and Chair Pose (Utkatasana) anchor you into the power of your legs while using your arms to open your chest and heart. These standing poses exercise both the sympathetic (fight-or-flight) and parasympathetic (relax-and-renew) systems and contribute to feelings of confidence and strength.

Any Warrior pose is particularly easy to adapt to work, as you can stand behind a chair or at your desk and practice as shown above. If someone asks what you are doing, you can calmly reply "just stretching."

For chair pose, simply rise from your chair halfway, align your body, and breathe fully for a few breaths. If your environment (or body) doesn't allow you to raise your arms comfortably, hold them by your side.

Energized and Powerful Voice

Chest openers tell your autonomic nervous system that you are safe. In these poses, you activate the throat's energy center, which is responsible for communication, self-expression, and the ability to speak your personal truth. Due to their physiological and psychological effects, chest-opening poses, also known as heart-opening poses, such as Cobra (Bhujangasana), Sphinx (Salamba Bhujangasana), Bow (Dhanurasana), and Camel (Ustrasana) can help you feel energized and create a powerful voice. These poses are designed to stretch and open the chest, shoulders, and front of the body, and can lead to increased vitality and a sense of rejuvenation. Chest openers facilitate deep, expansive breathing, increasing oxygen intake, which enhances lung capacity, oxygenates the blood, and leads to an energy boost. Chest-opening poses also can release tension and stress in the chest and shoulders. The physical act of opening the chest can have a psychological effect as well, because it symbolizes a willingness to be receptive, vulnerable, and open-minded. This psychological shift can translate into increased mental energy and a more positive outlook.

An at-work adaptation: Sitting in your chair in the seated easy pose adaptation or standing in mountain pose, clasping your hands behind your back. Remaining at ease and in alignment, breathe deeply and slowly as you broaden your collar bones, open your chest, and gaze upward. If you are standing and feel comfortable, extend your hands away from your body for a deeper stretch and chest opener.

Humility or Patience

Forward bends encourage the cultivation of patience through the combination of physical engagement and mental focus. They activate the parasympathetic nervous system (relax-and-renew) and down-regulate the sympathetic nervous system, invoking patience and humility. Standing forward bend (Uttanasana), wide-legged-forward bend (Prasarita Padottanasana), and child's pose (Balasana) lead to relaxation and a sense of calm. As you learn to patiently engage with your body, breath, and sensations, you cultivate a mindset that helps you navigate challenges with greater composure and resilience.

Forward bends are among the easiest poses for at-work adaption. Begin by standing in Tadasana, bringing awareness to alignment and breath. With feet flat on the floor, inhale while lengthening your body, then gently fold forward at your hip joints (the top part of your thigh, where the crease is), being careful to not strain your back or hamstrings. As illustrated below, you might place your hands on the back of your chair or a desk or bend your knees slightly to reduce strain. In the forward bend position, remain focused on your slow and deep inhalations and exhalations.

Release of Emotions or Cooling

Are you holding on to anger, hurt, or frustration? Humans hold a lot of emotions in our hips and our psoas, a muscle known as the "fight-flight" muscle. Although the primary focus of this section has been on the nervous system, one muscle that deserves special attention is the psoas.

The psoas (often referred to as the iliopsoas) is a deep-seated muscle that runs from the lower spine (specifically the lumbar vertebrae) through the pelvis and connects to the top of the femur (thigh bone). It connects the spine to the legs and plays an integral role in supporting the proper alignment of your spine. The psoas also enables you to maintain an appropriate posture, so if its functionality is impaired, you may experience back pain or discomfort. Its primary function is to flex the hip joint, which means it's responsible for lifting the thigh toward the torso. Additionally, the psoas muscle contributes to stabilizing the spine and pelvis during movement.

Although scientific research on the direct link between the psoas muscle and emotions is limited, neuroscience points to the psoas as a storage vessel of emotions. It is believed that the psoas muscle is intricately connected to the fight-or-flight response. When your nervous system senses danger, it alerts the psoas to fire up.

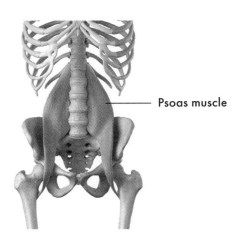
Psoas muscle

Some theories suggest that the body can remember emotional experiences and store them in physical structures like muscles. Due to its deep location and connection to the spine, it is thought the psoas could hold emotional memories or tensions. Continued stress causes the psoas to remain flexed, which continues the "You are not safe" communication between body and brain.

The psoas is one of the muscles that comprise the hip flexor group. Poses that stretch the hip flexor stretch and release the psoas, which help release tension and cool you down. When you first begin these hip-opening poses, you may be surprised to find an intense release of emotions.

Yoga poses such as Pigeon Pose (Eka Pada Rajakapotasana), Bound Angle Pose (Baddha Konasana), Low Lunge (Anjaneyasana), and Happy Baby Pose (Anadnda Balasana) all open and release the psoas and reduce the activation of the sympathetic (fight-or-flight) nervous system.

An easy adaptation for Bound Angle Pose is to sit in a chair, prop your feet on a block or box to elevate your feet, and bring the bottoms of your feet together. Notice the stretch in your hip flexors but be careful not to overextend or hurt your knees.

Another adaptation is to sit in your chair in Seated Easy Pose. Place your right ankle over your left knee with your right foot flexed. Maintaining posture and awareness, place your right hand on your right thigh (not your knee) and gently press down and forward to open the hip flexor. Maintain the posture for a few breaths, and then change legs.

BODY 103

Cleansing (Emotional or Physical)

If you feel emotionally exhausted fighting the fires of work or dealing with challenging situations, you might want to "cleanse" yourself of the feelings. Twists help you feel cleansed after emotional or physical releases. You can practice seated spinal twists, lying spinal twists, or standing spinal twists. Many standing and reclining poses have a revolved variation, including Revolved Triangle Pose (Parivrtta Trikonasana), Revolved Side Angle Pose (Parivrtta Parsvakonasana), or Bharadvaja's Twist (Bharadvajasana).

For an at-work adaptation, do seated twists in a chair, sitting comfortably with both sit bones toward the edge of the chair, your feet under your knees and your thighs parallel to the ground. In twists, it is important to not lead with the head. Keep your pelvis and hip straight and lengthen your spine. Keep your neck straight and relaxed and your head directly over your shoulders. Sit up tall, and on an inhalation, lengthen the spine. On the exhale, begin at the lower belly and twist toward one side. Continue lengthening and twisting slowly, with awareness. The head is the last body part to turn. Hold the full twist for a few slow, deep breaths, then repeat on the other side.

To Feel Balanced

The messages between your physical body and brain—both the thinking and emotional brain—are never-ending. Feeling physically out of balance affects your cognitive and emotional state. And when you feel emotionally or mentally unbalanced, it can be reflected in your physical abilities.

Daily activities, such as driving a vehicle, transporting physical equipment, carrying a baby on your hip, or simply how you sit, can result in your body feeling out of balance. Competing commands on your energy and attention can result in feeling emotionally and mentally out of balance. Also, you can feel out of balance if you have been giving too much or receiving too little (or vice versa). Balance poses help bring attention to where you are out of balance and help you regain equilibrium, both physically and energetically.

Tree pose (Vrksana) is one of the go-to yoga balance poses, but it isn't the only one. Nor is it an easy pose because it requires advanced attention to balance. Warrior 3 (Virabhadrasana III), side reclining leg lift (Anantasana), and alternating arms and leg extension in table pose are also beneficial for finding your balance, as is any pose standing on one leg. Tree pose can be readily available when in your office, even if your foot only rests on the side of your calf. If you need to be subtle, just stand on one leg to assess and regain your sense of balance.

Maintaining balance requires coordination of several muscle groups and sensory inputs. This coordination enhances the communication between the nervous system and muscles, leading to improved overall neuromuscular function. The focused attention required to maintain your balance also strengthens the mind-body connection, which can help reduce stress, improve overall mental well-being, and improve performance and effectiveness.

Releasing / Letting Go

It is not reasonable to expect any executive or leader (or any human) to go nonstop without taking the time to release and let go and allowing the mind and body to rejuvenate. Yet many leaders pride themselves on their relentless energy, but eventually it will be necessary to slow down and recharge. Rather than wait for a "big bang" moment to force you to stop (like my accident did for me), practicing restorative yoga poses provides invaluable benefits. While considered the least challenging, these poses may be the most powerful. Poses such as corpse pose (Savasana), child's pose (Balasana), and my personal favorite, legs-up-the-wall pose (Viparita Karani) are terrific at resetting the PNS (relax-and-renew).

By activating the parasympathetic nervous system, the body's relaxation response is engaged, leading to a decrease in stress hormones like cortisol and a reduction in overall stress. As a result, you may feel relaxed and calm, be mindful and aware, and have greater mental clarity and focus. Just five to ten minutes of any restorative yoga posture can provide immediate relief, but the real benefits are often cumulative. Regular practice helps you build resilience against the stresses of daily life.

Is Yoga the Only Answer?

Due to the amount of scientific study that supports the benefits of yoga and because these poses are easy to adapt in an office setting, I've introduced yoga poses that activate your parasympathetic nervous system and contribute to mindful success. However, there are alternative exercises and physical movements that can offer similar advantages. Qigong and tai chi, for instance, have demonstrated the ability to activate the parasympathetic nervous system. Engaging in mindful walking or stretching can also promote relaxation and transition your body into a parasympathetic mode.

Moreover, maintaining awareness of your posture and movement amplifies the impact on the parasympathetic nervous system. Regularly assuming postures such as mountain pose or seated easy pose—upright positions with relaxed shoulders—can become a habit. Similarly, integrating balance exercises such as standing on one leg slows you down and turns your focus inward. At the day's end, lying down with legs elevated against a wall can harness the benefits of an active parasympathetic system, including lowered blood pressure, stabilized mood, and heightened mental clarity.

In all these postures, slow and deep breathing engages the parasympathetic nervous system, fostering focused relaxation. The upcoming section will explore mindful breathing, a direct influencer of the autonomic nervous system that guides it toward a parasympathetic state.

Note that the yoga poses listed are just a few that offer a particular benefit. If you're interested in deeper practice or knowledge, consult a local or online yoga teacher, videos, or books to discover the poses that will best suit you.

Summary

Your body encompasses much more than just the skin, muscles, and vital organs that sustain you. Mindful attention to your body can influence your parasympathetic nervous system and transform the trajectory of reacting to life's events to achieve a state of balance, clarity, and concentration.

Taking care of the body, particularly the autonomic nervous system, can help you evolve from a mere successfully exhausted, task-oriented manager into an inspiring, effective, and health-conscious leader.

At the core of uniting the brain and body is the breath—a topic we will explore in the following section. Learning and practicing techniques for conscious breathing have the potential to revolutionize every facet of your life and contribute to your success as a mindfully successful leader.

And let me end this section with a final note of caution: always consult your medical provider before beginning an exercise program, especially if you have any physical conditions or concerns. Even the most well-trained yoga teacher is not intended to replace conventional care or as a reason to postpone consulting a health care provider about a medical problem.

CHAPTER 4

BREATH

Have you ever taken a moment to ponder the profound significance of the breath? Perhaps not because this potent, life-sustaining force requires no consciousness or active contemplation. So why would I dedicate an entire section to the topic of breath?

Here is why: your breath obviously keeps you alive—but consciously harnessed, it also is capable of swiftly reshaping your entire energetic state and thus your life.

Breathing is so much more than the lungs taking in oxygen and releasing carbon dioxide—it's a profound tool that can awaken your parasympathetic nervous system. It can contribute to emotional regulation, improved focus, reduce stress, and lower blood pressure. The magic doesn't stop there—it holds the key to tranquility within your limbic system. With each *deliberate* breath, you wield the power to reimagine your mental landscape and guide your physical reactions. The art of harnessing breath—a simple yet astonishing feat—will help you command your thoughts and bodily sensations in more productive, healthy ways.

As mentioned in the introduction, breathing techniques helped Leigh, a director in a management consulting company near Washington, DC, overcome her anxiety about an three-day strategic off-site retreat. The company she was working with had grown impressively over a few years, difficult conversations were needed, and the leaders she worked with were distrustful. During a coaching conversation before the retreat, we reviewed the power tool of using breath in high-stress situations.

"Remember your breathing techniques," I said during a coaching conversation. I reminded her of two breathing techniques—one to calm her down (4-4-7) and another (alternative nostril breathing) to increase her feelings of balance. (Both techniques are described later in this section.)

After the retreat, Leigh expressed wonderment at how the simple breathing exercises effectively calmed her down and instilled confidence to have difficult conversations. The breathing techniques energized her ability to help leaders shape strategic decisions that would allow the company to prosper. Her anxious feelings about the retreat shifted so much that Leigh later reported the experience as "revitalizing and inspiring."

Many people don't realize that the way you breathe can generate angry feelings—or that conscious breathing can help dissipate anger. Your breath can contribute to feeling distracted and scattered, or it can help you focus and generate clear thinking. Breath can contribute to irritability and depression, or it can carry you toward calm and moderation. Breath connects the mind—part of the brain—and the body.

David, the high-level military officer introduced in the Brain section, effectively used breathing techniques with meditation to reduce the negative influence of growing up in a highly dysfunctional environment. Sam, the regional director of a multinational corporation, and Pat, CEO of a consulting company who was fighting a legal assault from the CEO of another company—and a former friend—integrated breathing techniques to calm the sympathetic nervous system (fight-or-flight) and stimulate the parasympathetic nervous system (relax-and-renew). Endless other leaders—me included—have incorporated the simple power of "Take a breath" to initiate calm and boost self-confidence.

Before I learned about the intricacies and nuances of the breath's influence on our mind, body, and emotional states, I would have assumed that tension and stress resulted in shallow breathing or holding my breath. Relaxing would mean my breath would be slow and even.

As I mentioned in the first chapter, my thinking was backward. I was tense *because* I was holding my breath or breathing quickly. I was calm and relaxed *because* I was breathing fully.

"Take a Breath"

If you can, stop for a moment and notice your breath. Really tune in. What movements and sensations do you discern as you breathe? Is your breath shallow, confined mainly to the upper chest? Or do you sense its depth as it fills your lower rib cage and belly? Are your inhalations and exhalations steady and balanced? As you breathe, contemplate the fact that your breath is more than a life-sustaining force—it's a vital and potent tool.

Remember—unlike the body's other visceral functions (digestion, endocrine, cardiovascular), you can voluntarily regulate the breath. As I wrote earlier, the "thinking brain" cannot consciously command the heartbeat to slow or thoughts to cease. However, directing the breath makes both possible. That is why the US military, including the Navy SEALs and air force fighter pilots, includes breathing techniques in its training for high-stress situations to help regulate stress management and overall wellness.

As you can see, it's worth contemplating the many facets of breath. Not only is breathing essential to stay alive, but it also can enhance your sense of "aliveness." It has the potential to improve your well-being in ways you may not have thought of before.

My introduction to the power of the breath came in the anteroom of a yoga studio in Arlington. In the beginning, it was a rocky relationship. As I waited for my beginners' yoga class to start, I ferociously scanned the book selection. Noticing my own agitation, I commanded myself to "calm down." I couldn't quite get there.

Experience had taught me that answers to problems could almost always be found in a book. I scanned. I paced. The music in my mind rose to a crescendo. I just needed to find the *right* book. I picked up this book and that one, then another, again and again. None of the titles seemed to contain the answer to a question so vague I couldn't even articulate it. I felt lost, my mind awash in frustration and confusion.

Sensing my agitation, Mark, my yoga teacher, asked, "Is there something I can help you find?"

"I don't know," I replied tersely. "Life just sucks, and I'm sure I can find an answer here if I keep looking."

From behind the desk, he looked at me calmly.

"Breathe," he said gently. "Just breathe."

At that moment, all I could hear was my heart pounding. His response felt dismissive. I was forty years old, recently divorced from a man who'd beaten me up. In the wake of our divorce, I was desperately trying to recover financially from my business failures in addition to supporting two children in out-of-state colleges.

The feeling of being dismissed took me back to the night my former husband had thrown me against a wall and began choking me, his strong hands squeezing my neck and pounding my head into the wall. Now I felt even more agitated. I had serious problems to fix! And this smug little jerk with a big belly in yoga shorts was telling me to *breathe*?

Breathe? I yelled at him in my mind. *You want me to* breathe? *If I weren't breathing, I'd be lying on the floor unconscious. How the hell is breathing going to solve my mountain of problems?*

If it hadn't been one more indication of failure, I would have stormed out of the yoga studio right then. Instead, fighting back tears and feeling humiliated, I entered the studio for the class and took a yoga mat in the far back corner.

Like many of life's threshold moments, the significance of that moment would take me years to understand. Mark's simple advice—"Breathe"—began a journey that altered the trajectory of my life. I found Mark's word "dismissive" because I didn't understand the power of his directive. Back then, breath was breath. And even if I had thought about my breathing, I didn't realize it could control or influence how I felt.

In yoga classes, sometimes, it felt like I was forcing myself into a pose as my body responded with a resounding "No!" I noticed I was often holding my breath.

"Step into warrior pose and just notice," Mark would say patiently. "Slowly and fully inhale; release and let go as you exhale." With time, I learned how using my breath could help my body relax into a pose.

BREATH 113

And then I realized the breathing techniques were just as useful off the yoga mat.

The message really hit home for me while riding on the back of my husband's Harley-Davidson motorcycle. On our first road trip after a nasty accident the prior year, we entered a right turn, like the one had led to the accident, and I instinctively gasped and held my breath. Calling on what I had learned, I consciously exhaled as we entered those curves and followed that with a long, peaceful inhale as we exited the turn. With each deep, mindful breath, my body relaxed. I stopped clenching my muscles in anticipation of a fall that never came.

The realization that I could relax my body and release my mind by channeling my breath felt miraculous. Could changing my breathing help me recover from the trauma of the motorcycle accident? I decided to carry that knowledge with me and experiment in my everyday life. When entering a meeting that I considered high-stakes—with my boss, a prospective client, or a potentially tense conversation with an employee—I began to check in with my breath. Was I exhaling completely and inhaling fully?

This can work for you, too. Instead of charging into a meeting ready for battle, conscious breathing can enable you to enter calmly and confidently. Instead of risking overreactions due to a hypervigilant, distracted mental state, mindful breathing can help you control your emotions and mental state. Deep, intentional breaths can serve as a silent, invisible tool, ultimately enhancing your ability to be a more impactful, authentic leader.

How I breathed could initiate an incredible transformation in how I functioned as a leader. Just like I'd delved into the working of the brain and the body, I pursued an in-depth study of breath and learned how breathing techniques affected the brain and body. While the physical structure to support the breath is complex and intricate, what I learned—and what I help leaders to learn and remember—is that the ways you breathe can help you perform more effectively and with ease. I'll introduce simple techniques later in the chapter that will enhance your ability to be mindfully successful. For example:

- To feel calm and relaxed—exhale longer than you inhale.
- To feel invigorated and energized—inhale longer than you exhale.
- To feel balanced and grounded—inhale and exhale for equal durations.
- Shallow breathing from your upper chest tells your body you are in danger!
- Deep, steady breathing from your lower ribs and belly tells your body all is well.

I recently received a call from Leigh, the management consulting company director, introduced at the beginning of this section, who proudly told me she had been promoted to vice president within her company. She shared a story about facilitating a "fireside chat" with a senior federal government executive in front of an audience of two hundred government and industry leaders at the American Council for Technology (ACT) and Industry Advisory Council (IAC) conference.

Knowing that being an influential public speaker was one of her goals, I asked how she felt the facilitation went. "It went great!" she exclaimed and credited breathing exercises with exponentially elevating her performance. "I used the alternative nostril breathing beforehand, and I was completely comfortable. I know there are areas in which I'll do better next time, but I think it went extremely well."

I asked how speaking publicly in a high-profile, high-stakes environment was different when she was focused on the other speaker and her audience rather than herself.

With a confident smile, she replied, "Wonderful! It's amazing what a little bit of breathing can do for you."

The Three Diaphragms

What is the science behind something so subtle, but so incredibly influential, in helping you drive the lasting change crucial to mindful success? This rudimentary drawing of the human skeleton system can help you understand more clearly how breathing works when I describe the three diaphragms model.*

In the lower part of the body, the journey begins with the pelvis, which serves as the body's foundation. Extending outward from the pelvis are the hip bones on either side. Moving down from the hip bones are the thigh bones, the shins, and the ankles. Finally, at the end of the progression are your feet.

---

* As referenced by Matthew Taylor, PhD, physical therapist, experienced registered yoga teacher (E-RYT), and a leading author on incorporating yoga therapy into traditional rehabilitations. https://matthewjtaylor.com.

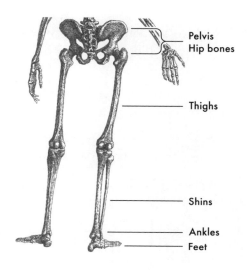

Moving to the upper part of the body, the journey starts just above the pelvis. Here are five lumbar vertebrae, twelve thoracic vertebrae connected to the ribs, and your collar bones. Above the collar bones are seven cervical vertebrae, which bear the weight of a ten-to-twelve-pound head.

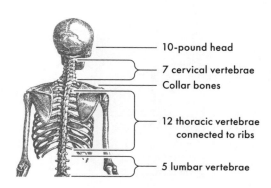

And all these 206 to 213 bones make up the adult human body.

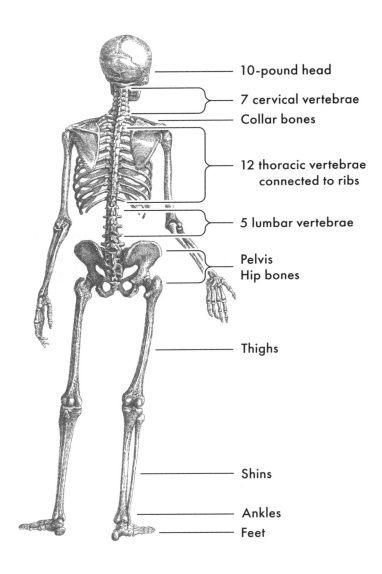

- 10-pound head
- 7 cervical vertebrae
- Collar bones
- 12 thoracic vertebrae connected to ribs
- 5 lumbar vertebrae
- Pelvis
- Hip bones
- Thighs
- Shins
- Ankles
- Feet

Added to the model are the three diaphragms, which include the respiratory, pelvic, and cervical–thoracic diaphragms.

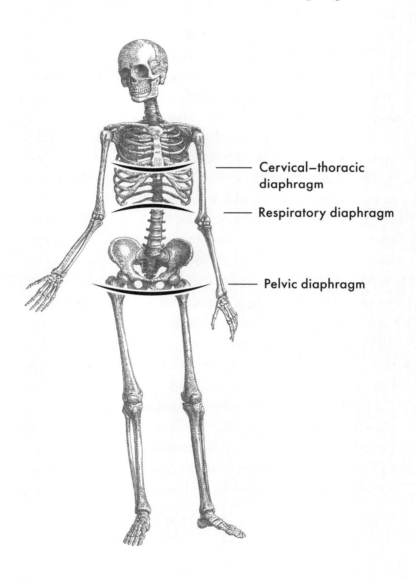

You most likely are familiar with the respiratory diaphragm, which goes across the bottom of the rib cage, separating the heart and lungs from the internal organs. When the respiratory diaphragm contracts, it pulls down to create increased spacing in the rib cage, which fills with air. A second diaphragm is called the pelvic diaphragm because it contains the pelvic floor muscles. The respiratory diaphragm and the pelvic diaphragms are in constant movement, working in rhythm.

The third diaphragm is the cervical-thoracic diaphragm, considered a critical backup system when extra air is needed, where the muscles of the neck and the chest lift on the rib cage to increase the space for additional air.

How you breathe matters! Remember that people typically take 12 to 15 breaths per minute. That adds up to 900 breaths per hour and 17,000 per day (some estimates are as high as 17,280 to 28,800 per day). When you practice slow, deep breathing from the respiratory diaphragm, you activate your parasympathetic nervous system, which is responsible for relaxation and renewal. This signals that you are safe, leading to reduced perception of pain, a more optimized immune system, improved mood regulation, and clear, focused mental clarity.

Conversely, shallow breathing from the cervical-thoracic diaphragm activates your sympathetic nervous system, responsible for the fight-or-flight-or-freeze. Shallow breathing can result in hypervigilance, scattered thoughts, irritability or depression, increased blood pressure, and fatigue due to disrupted sleep patterns.

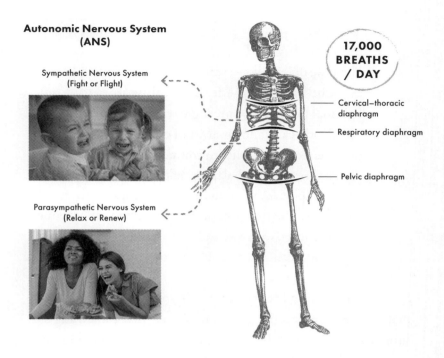

I studied yoga regularly for many years and had the good fortune to take teacher training with Doug Keller, who, in addition to teaching in the northern Virginia area, trains internationally. Doug is well known for his extensive writing on yoga topics in magazines and journals. Among his many books is *Refining the Breath*. He has also served as a distinguished professor at the Maryland University of Integrative Health in their master's degree program in yoga therapy.

Doug writes:

> What we observe concerning the quality of our in-breath and out-breath provides a revealing mirror of our habitual (and often unrecognized) stance toward life. The depth, ease, and comfort of our inhalation reflects our openness and ability to embrace life in the moment; the quality of our inhalation reflects our readiness and consent to participate in life as it unfolds before and within us. The freedom of our exhalation reflects our ability to let go with ease and understanding and to move on; it shows our trust in life that loosens or overcomes.[*]

Understanding the intricacies of your body's diaphragmatic systems reveals the profound impact that something as fundamental as breathing has on your overall well-being. By mastering the art of mindful breathing, harnessing the power of the respiratory, pelvic, and cervical-thoracic diaphragms, you can cultivate a state of relaxation and mental clarity. This awareness empowers you to drive lasting change and achieve mindful success. Whether it's reducing stress, enhancing mood, or improving sleep, the simple act of deep, diaphragmatic breathing serves as a cornerstone for a healthier, more balanced life. Embrace the science of breath, and let it guide you toward a more mindful and fulfilling existence.

---

[*] Doug Keller, *Refining the Breath: Pranayama: The Art of the Awakened Breath* (Do Yoga Productions, 2018).

Breathing Practices

Mindful breathing, ensuring you breathe deeply and fully, is a simple first step of becoming conscious of its effects on mind and body. In addition, you can learn breathing techniques that will trigger specific, desired responses: when it's beneficial to eject tension, stress, frustration, or anger from your body; if you need to feel energized; if you're trying to exercise your parasympathetic nervous systems regularly; or for balancing the mind.

Basic rules about breathing to remember are the following:

- Breathing practices that make your inhalations longer than your exhalations are stimulating.
- Breathing practices that make your exhalations longer than your inhalations are calming.
- Breathing practices that make your inhalations and exhalations equal lengths are considered "balancing."
- Shallow breathing from your upper chest tells your body you're in danger.
- Deep, steady breathing from the lower ribs and belly tell your body all is well.

When you want to feel energized, focus on longer inhalations than exhalations; to feel calm, focus on longer exhalations than inhalations; and to feel balanced, focus on equal-length inhalations and exhalations.

In the following pages, I'll introduce suggestions for breathing practices that you can call upon as needed.

Disclaimer: The information provided is for educational purposes only and does not substitute for professional medical advice. Consult with a health-care professional before beginning any new exercise program.

Do not participate in intense breathing exercises without consulting your physician if you have asthma, diabetes, epilepsy, or a heart condition without consulting your physician.

* * *

To Feel Calmed and Reduce Anxiety—4-4-7 Breathing

Exhalations longer than your inhalations are calming.
The 4-4-7 (or 4-7-8) breathing technique is the go-to exercise I first introduce to my clients because it is easy to do and can be practiced anywhere and at any time without anyone knowing you are doing it. And the calming results are immediate!

The technique is based on the ancient yogic practice of controlling your breath, called pranayama. When you first begin, try to practice twice a day for only four cycles. After you get used to it, you can work up to seven or eight cycles.

The basic premise of the practice is to exhale longer than you inhale and pause between the inhale and exhale.

1. Find a comfortable position to sit, stand, or lie with your back straight.

2. Place your tongue against the back of your top teeth, and keep it there during the breathing practice. This helps to refrain from clenching or tightening your jaws.
3. Begin with a complete exhalation.
4. Inhale through your nose for a count of four.
5. Pause or lightly hold your breath for a count of four.
6. Exhale completely for a count of seven or eight.
7. This completes one cycle. Repeat for three to seven more cycles, then return your breath to normal.

Note the intent is to breathe slowly and with ease, so don't rush the count or vigorously hold your breath. Slowly inhale, lightly pause, and slowly exhale.

You can also practice this during your work commute. Call upon this practice before a high-stress event or during a meeting at which you want to be at peak performance. This breathing technique is also soothing if you wake up at night with your mind racing about past or future events—lie still and practice.

To Return Breathing to Normal after Stressful Experience — Box Breathing

Inhalations and exhalations of equal lengths are balancing.
Box breathing is a simple, powerful technique to return breathing to its normal rhythm after a stressful experience. As referenced earlier, Box Breathing is widely used by US Navy SEALs, air force pilots, and first responders. Like the 4-4-7 technique, it can be done anywhere at any time, including at your work desk, or standing in a public place.

1. Find a comfortable position to sit, stand, or lie with your back straight.
2. Inhale slowly and fully through your nose while counting to four.
3. Lightly hold or pause your breath for a count of four, keeping your jaws unclenched and face relaxed.
4. Slowly exhale for four seconds.
5. Lightly hold or pause for four seconds.
6. Repeat the process three to eight times.

When you first begin the practice, you may find the four-count is too strenuous, in which case you can begin with a three-count. As you become more experienced with the method, you may extend the count to five or six.

The intent is to breathe slowly and with ease, so don't hurriedly rush the count, vigorously hold your breath, or compete to see how long of count you can attain. Slowly inhale, lightly pause, slowly exhale, lightly pause, and repeat.

To Feel Energized and Relieve Anger — Lion's Breath (Simhasana)

Exhalations longer than your inhalations are calming.
Lion's Breath is energetic and awakens the body in ways that relieve tension, stress, frustration, and anger. It may look and feel silly, but it is a beautiful way to introduce ease and remind you not to take yourself too seriously. It also opens the throat energy center and helps to boost confidence.

1. Lion's breath is typically done kneeling with the ankles crossed but can be done standing or sitting.
2. Place your hands on your knees. Inhale through your nose with your mouth closed.
3. Open your mouth wide, and stick out your tongue as much as possible. Exhale forcefully through your mouth, with a "haaaah" sound from the back of your throat.
4. Try bringing your internal focus toward the center of your forehead or the tip of your nose as you exhale.
5. Inhale, returning to a neutral face and posture.
6. Repeat three to six times. If your ankles are crossed, change the position halfway through the practice.

To Feel Balanced and Activate Both Sides of Your Brain—Alternate Nostril Breathing (Nadi Shodhana)

Inhalations and exhalations of equal lengths are balancing. Alternate nostril breathing is descriptive—you breathe slowly through one nostril while gently holding the other shut with your fingers, then swap nostrils and repeat. Once you experience the benefits of this breathing technique, you're likely to call upon it regularly to benefit from its calming effects. This breathing technique induces a state of calm, eases stress, and reduces anxiety. It also improves brain function, including helping with memory and movement.

1. You can practice this technique in any seated position.
2. Position your right hand so that your pointer and middle fingers are folded into your palm, leaving your thumb, ring finger, and pinky sticking up.
3. Bring your thumb to the right side of your nose and your ring finger to the left.
4. Inhale and exhale once regularly to prepare.
5. Close off your right nostril with your thumb.
6. Slowly and fully inhale through your left nostril.
7. Close off your left nostril with your ring finger.
8. Open your right nostril as you slowly exhale through your right nostril.
9. Close off your right nostril with your thumb.
10. Open and slowly exhale through your left nostril.
11. Slowly inhale through your left nostril.
12. Try to work up to doing at least ten rounds. However, at first, you might only make it through a few rounds of this breath.

If your mind wanders, focus on counting the length of your inhales and exhales or the sensation of your breath on the skin under your nose. It may feel relaxed as you inhale and warm as you exhale. And if you ever begin to feel light-headed, release both nostrils and breathe normally.

When people first begin, the most uncomfortable part of this breathing technique is the awkwardness of using your hand to your face. Fortunately, the benefits of this breathing technique can be gained without using your hands by simply focusing on which nostril you are inhaling and exhaling.

A word of caution: If you are a little congested, expect this breathing practice to move the mucus out, so have some tissues handy. However, if you are too stuffed up to breathe out of either nostril, you won't be able to get the intended benefits, so wait until the air passageways are clear to do this exercise.

To Feel Calm *or* to Feel Energized (Viloma Breathing)

While the other breathing techniques introduced can generally be easily done, Viloma Breathing, also known as "interrupted breathing," "wave breath," and three-part breathing, may require more focus and awareness when you first begin the practice. However, as with all breathing techniques listed here, the benefits can be immense. Once you are familiar with doing the three-part breathing practice, you can do it almost anywhere.

Viloma Breathing involves deliberately pausing or interrupting the natural flow of inhalation and exhalation. The specific impact of pausing during inhalation or exhalation can vary from person to person. However, in general, pausing during **exhalation** produces **calming and relaxing** effects, while pausing during **inhalation** can be more **invigorating and energizing**.

It is important to note that everyone may have varying responses to these effects, and the impact of Viloma Breathing can be influenced by factors such as your unique physiology, the broader context of your practice, and your personal inclinations. Consequently, I encourage you to explore both approaches and attentively observe how your body and mind react. As with any breath control practice, it's essential to practice mindfully and listen to your body to determine what works best for you in different situations.

It is suggested you start with a short practice, perhaps five to ten minutes. As you become more comfortable with the technique and are more familiar with the effects it has on you, you may extend the duration of the practice to fifteen to twenty minutes or longer if desired.

1. Sit or lie comfortably with your spine straight in a relaxed position.
2. Close your eyes if you are comfortable.
3. Begin with normal, steady breathing for a few rounds.

4. **To Feel Energized**
   Inhalations longer than your exhalations are stimulating.
   a. On your next inhalation, inhale into your upper chest and pause; then inhale into your rib cage and pause; then continue the inhalation into your belly. These pauses should be natural and not forced.
   b. After completing the inhalation into your belly, exhale without interruptions.
   c. Continue this pattern—inhale, pause; inhale into rib cage, pause; inhale into belly, pause; then continuous release.

5. **To Feel Calm**
   Exhalations longer than your inhalations are calming.
   a. Inhale fully through your upper chest, rib cage, and belly for one continuous inhalation. Pause.
   b. As you begin your exhalation, exhale one-third of the air, pause; exhale another third of the air, pause, and continue exhaling fully. These pauses should be natural and not forced.
   c. After completing the exhalation, inhale without interruption.
   d. Continue this pattern—exhale one-third, pause; exhale another third, pause; exhale fully.

6. When you're ready to conclude your Viloma Breathing practice, return to normal, natural breathing for a few breaths.
7. When you are ready, open your eyes if they were closed and gently transition to your next activity.

Summary

Ah, the power of the breath!

It can be difficult to truly comprehend that what all living humans do—breathe—can have such an astounding impact. But I urge you to try. As executives and senior leaders who are making high-stakes, potentially life-altering decisions, harnessing the breath can be your "special sauce" to foster clear thinking, a calm mind, and balanced brain activity.

If you want people to work with and for you, tune into your breath and notice that there will be a more inviting feel around you. People will respect you and perhaps be in awe, and less fearful that you are going to unleash your anger toward them. As you reflect about work events at the end of the day, you can do so with peace and awareness rather than endless questioning, regrets, or self-doubt.

Don't be like Michael, the CEO introduced at the beginning of this book, who insulted and ridiculed the VP. Instead, learn from David, the colonel who learned how to embrace, rather than fight, his emotional brain. He became a more effective, inspiring, and peaceful leader by accepting and embracing the leadership positions and opportunities that he had. Or learn from Karl, the technically brilliant VP who incorporated breathing and brain-training techniques to lead more successfully, with greater ease and more positive impact, and was promoted to senior vice president in his company. Or be like Pat, the CEO and majority owner of a $250 million company, who was fighting business sabotage from a former partner, who used breathing techniques to develop previously untapped resources, which helped her stave off the attempted takeover and expand the business.

These leaders and endless others used the combined power of the breath, together with their brains and bodies, to overcome obstacles and be more influential, mindfully successful leaders.

CHAPTER 5

THE INTEGRATION

When integrated, understanding the brain's intricacies, embracing the interconnected dynamics of our body and nervous system, and harnessing the transformative potential of controlled breathing become powerful tools for creating mindful success. Living in regular awareness of your actions, thoughtfully making choices that serve you well, and mastering your emotional responses empower you to more effectively carry out the functional skills you have accumulated over the years.

The act of extending grace, to yourself and those around you, amplifies the positive impact of these practices. Throughout this book, I have provided illustrations of the profound transformations my clients have achieved through meditation, deliberate physical alignment, and mindful breathwork. These strategies hold the same potential for a positive shift in your life.

While the book details the tips and techniques of brain, body, and breath, the real magic happens when these are integrated. How does this integral approach harmonize and fuel your journey toward mindful success? It's about leveraging *awareness* to shape your actions and *discerning* the ripple effects on yourself, those around you, and the organizations in which you work. This knowledge has the power to be a true catalyst, changing your life for the better.

Let's look at Chris, senior director of engineering for an international technology company. He led a team of highly talented engineers and developers responsible for building and managing the technical design and development of the company's flagship product.

Mindfully Successful Chris

Chris had invested a lot of energy and hard work to earn his position. He loved leading the engineering functions and relished the opportunity to develop and support the employees he worked with. Chris understood the brain's power and learned to harness its emotional and thinking aspects. He practiced meditation throughout the years, and frequently used the noticing and naming techniques introduced in the Brain section. Tapping into body awareness and the power of the breath had helped Chris as he climbed the career ladder. He would describe himself as mindfully successful rather than successfully exhausted.

One day, I received a call from Chris, who sounded uncharacteristically frazzled and out of sorts.

"I have a big challenge," he said, "and I'd like you to help me process what's going on and how I should handle it."

Chris described one of the more painful parts of his job. The company's board had replaced the CEO, who had a technology and engineering background, with a CEO who was grounded in finance. The new CEO's leadership model was unemotional detachment, and he tended to view the company through a purely financial lens and mandated a companywide 10 percent reduction in workforce.

"Make it happen," the CEO told his team, including Chris.

To Chris and other leaders in the company, the draconian approach was overly severe and bordering on cruel. Chris initially saw only two choices, following the CEO's orders or finding a new job. Finally, he decided on a third option: making the changes as mindfully as possible to best serve the company and the employees—whom he saw as individuals, not just as a body count.

After he and the other directors and executives determined which positions to eliminate or combine, which employees would be affected, and other logistical matters such as the date and method for announcing the reductions in force, Chris knew he needed a mindful approach to the layoffs.

In college, Chris had been a distance track runner, and post-college, he had adopted the hobby of mountain climbing. He recalled how he had prepared for his athletic events and reflected on our coaching engagement, where I had suggested approaching leadership as he would run a marathon or compete in a triathlon.

Chris knew he must begin by leading himself and getting "in shape" for the challenge ahead. He recalled being fired from a job during college and the devastating feeling he was left with—not good enough, embarrassed, complete failure. Refreshing his memory on what he knew about the brain and his emotional triggers, rather than suppressing these feelings from the past or "talking himself calm," he practiced Naming and Scratch the Record when he noticed these emotions surfacing.

He committed to meditating daily for at least ten minutes rather than relying on his inconsistent practice of longer meditations. Chris knew he needed his brain, mind, and thoughts to be in top shape for a painful event that would affect hundreds of families.

Chris also recognized that stress was taking a physical toll. Recalling how his physical positions affected his autonomic nervous system, he paid conscious attention to how he sat, stood, and walked. Was he telling his body "Danger, danger," or was he reassuring his body that he was safe? He incorporated a ten-minute daily yoga practice and included standing poses to help him feel strong, chest-opening poses to energize and help him speak with confidence, and forward bends to support humility and patience.

As the layoff announcement approached, even with all his preparation, he felt slightly depressed. He knew he couldn't change outcomes or save employees about to lose their jobs. Instead, he set an intention to reduce the negative impacts of the situation as mindfully as possible.

Just before his 8:30 a.m. meeting with the HR representative and those being notified that they were being let go, he practiced a few rounds of alternative nostril breathing to activate both sides of his brain, feel centered, and foster. Entering the room, he sensed that employees understood why they were there. Employing the communication skills he had acquired over his decades of experience, he took a deep breath, followed by a long exhalation before he spoke.

I spoke with Chris a few days later. "How did it go, and how are you?"

"Well," he replied, "I did what I could do to support them and myself. I realize that we [the leadership team executing the layoffs] had weeks to process it, and those laid off were at the beginning of the process. I hope I've been the kind of leader they deserve."

Successfully Exhausted Chris

Contrast Chris's response with how he likely would have responded without understanding and using the powers of his brain, body, and breath to be mindfully successful. We will call this version Chris 2. Based on my experience, I can imagine a scenario something like this:

Chris 2 was told must reduce his workforce by 10 percent. His amygdala fired off "Danger, danger!" based on his experience of being fired during college. Unaware of what was happening in his brain, he attempted to force his emotional brain to be silent. He retreated into the habitual, highly cognitive functioning that he believed had served him so well. After all, he was a senior director.

At home that same evening, he was in a foul mood, felt out of control, and repeatedly told himself to calm down. His wife and kids needed his time and attention, but his mind was back at work. How could he do this? Who should go? Was he likely to be next?

A customarily reserved guy, Chris 2 retreated further into his instinctual introversion. He would figure it out by gathering data as he and the other executives determined which positions to eliminate or combine. He really hated this part of the job.

As the weeks dragged on between the CEO's mandate and the date of announcing the layoffs, Chris 2 found himself snapping at employees and his family. He knew intellectually it wasn't their fault, and he felt like he was constantly tamping down a scream of frustration! This mandate also meant extra hours at his computer trying to create a plan, which interrupted his exercise routine.

And his sleep was suffering because of constant worry. How could he minimize the number of people eliminated and still meet the 10 percent reduction? Perhaps he should let the higher-paid engineers go and hope the newer engineers would step up. How was he supposed to keep up with the ever-demanding work commitments with fewer people? Was he making the right choices? And if he wasn't, would he be next?

On the day of the formal announcements, he was at his office at 6:30 a.m., poring over the lists one last time and fretting. Were these the right people? Was his own job in jeopardy? As he entered the 8:30 a.m. meeting with the HR representative, he could sense that those called to the meeting understood why they were there. "I've done all I can do," he told himself.

The stress of worrying that he would be next took its toll on Chris 2. He decided that rather than wait for them to fire him, he was going to take control and quit the company he had worked for most of his adult life. He knew he would find something else where he wouldn't feel as threatened. For Chris 2, the fight-or-flight response won out, and he decided on flight.

Mindfully Successful Chris—Continued

Chris carried out the initial 10 percent reduction successfully. However, the layoffs marked only the initial phase of cost reduction; subsequently, there was further amplification toward cost reduction, with a logical progression toward an enterprise-wide consolidation. With Chris's proven engineering and leadership skills and his abilities with finance and resource models, he found himself very much in the thick of things as the final organizational change was decided at the corporate level. He was selected by corporate to lead the massive enterprise consolidation of engineering functions.

Chris recalled what he had learned from a former VP who often said, "You're no good if you're exhausted; in fact, you're probably dangerous." Before jumping in to accept the opportunity, Chris asked for a week off to consider what this would entail for him, his now very large team, and the company.

After a week spent in nature, walking in the woods, fishing in the rivers, meditating under the stars, and talking with his spouse, he decided to accept the challenge.

As he says, the train had left the station, and he could lead, follow, or get out of the way. His contemporaries were telling him they needed him, in part because he was the engineer most versed in finance, but mostly because he was most calm. He described himself as very measured, controlled, and paced. "I knew it was a lot like endurance sports," he recalled.

And so, he began the triathlon of leading the consolidation initiative for four years. To say it was difficult was an understatement.

Ripping functions embedded at the business level and consolidating them at the enterprise level entailed creating a whole new organization. Yet despite the chaos of process changes, frustrated employees, and the ever-present pressure of cost savings, the business was expected to continue high production levels.

Despite being as mindful as possible, Chris's overall health was negatively impacted because of stress. Even so, he knew he was in much better shape—both during the consolidation and after—than many might have been.

Because of the years of meditation, physical yoga, and breathing practices, his brain and body were conditioned to process external events from a healthier perspective. "I'd come into a meeting, going a hundred miles per hour, walk in and look around. After a deep inhalation and heavy, clearing exhalation, I would say to myself, 'Now we can get down to business.'"

He adjusted his schedule so he could tack on a visit to the fitness center at the end of the day, even though he often had more work to do at home after dinner. And on most days at the office, he would go outside for a twenty-to-thirty-minute walk at lunch, engaging in the Noticing exercise described in the Brain section of this book.

"My day is filled with decisions, often having far-reaching impact. It was helpful for me to practice noticing without judgment as a regular practice so I could be more effective at—and yes mindful of—the decisions I made," Chris explained.

As Chris described his role during the organizational restructuring, I commented that he sounded like he was a very inspirational leader. "I don't know that they would call me an inspiring leader. I think the people I worked for—my subordinates and peers—were appreciative and respectful. They were glad I was out there doing the job that needed to be done, shielding them, and running interference so they could stay focused on creating products. When I said, 'I need some help,' they knew I needed it and readily provided it. I guess I would describe my leadership as judicious and mindful."

"When you think about that period now, what goes on for you?" I asked Chris a few years after his retirement.

After a thoughtful pause, Chris replied, "I guess relief. I'm glad it's over. I left the place better than I found it. I have a clear conscience, knowing that I did everything I could, put in my best effort, and didn't shirk my duty."

"Why did you stick it out?" I asked.

"I'm glad I could do it, because there were other people who couldn't have done it. I was driven by consciousness and acted on principle. If I could not articulate what the driving principle was, I needed to rethink what I was doing."

Summary

Being a leader is tough. It necessitates the delicate art of precisely handling day-to-day imperatives while juggling organizational goals, focusing on outpacing the competition and orchestrating strategic direction. A leader must draw upon an arsenal of skills cultivated through experience and education. Leadership often requires relentless hard work, perseverance, and unwavering commitment.

Yet along with these demands, leadership also offers the promise of great rewards. through understanding the inner workings of your brain, your body, your breath, and the many tools at your disposal, you can discover ways to positively impact those under your guidance. Armed with insights and practices, you can effectively navigate the demanding aspects of your leadership role while preserving your well-being and inner peace. This inevitably leaves an indelible, constructive influence on those around you.

Which Chris would you prefer to be? Which Chris would you prefer to work for or with? The power of being mindfully successful lies in its ability to sculpt the trajectory of your actions and reshape the decisions you make and the ways you implement those decisions. While it may not always change the immediate, tangible outcomes—such as employees facing unemployment—it undoubtedly redefines the broader impact it has on leaders like Chris and the context they influence.

In the journey to mindful success, it's essential to recognize that the initial positive effects may seem subtle. As you persist, these transformations become second nature, and the neurological and physiological shifts occur effortlessly, demanding little conscious effort.

You might begin with a weekly yoga class or an "as-needed" breathing exercise. Over time, recognizing the slow improvement in how you think or feel, you might increase the mindfulness practices. When you experience an amygdala hijack, you might be able to recognize what is happening rather than let the hijack take over. Or you might begin by employing techniques such as noticing, naming, or scratching the record.

You are creating your life one thought at a time, one step at a time, one small, safe experiment at a time. I will close with the words of Lao Tzu, an extraordinary thinker during the sixth century BCE and generally considered the founder of Taoism.

Watch your thoughts; they become your words,
watch your words; they become your actions,
watch your actions; they become your habits,
watch your habits; they become your character,
watch your character; it becomes your destiny.

ACKNOWLEDGMENTS

First and foremost, thanks to my incredible husband, Mark, who is my partner in every aspect of life. Without your unwavering encouragement and support, many first (and second) draft reads, and constantly stretching my ideas and approach, this book would not be where it is now. I am deeply grateful for you and all that you do.

To my daughter and cherished thought partner, Nicole, whose insightful conversations and early reading were instrumental in shaping and articulating my ideas—thank you for helping me bring my thoughts and ideas into the world. I also want to thank Danny and Micah for their continuous encouragement, genuine curiosity, and thoughtful questioning, which challenged and refined my thoughts. Your support has been invaluable in bringing this work to fruition.

My brother, Robert, gave me unwavering support and encouragement during my childhood and shaped my love for learning and curiosity. He patiently answered my endless childish questions, fostering a sense of wonder that has stayed with me. One never truly knows the profound impact they have on others.

I cannot thank my editor and friend, Maren Showkeir, enough! Without Maren's invaluable guidance, unwavering support, and exceptional talent, this book would merely be fragmented thoughts running through my mind and disjointed words stored on my computer. Namaste and with much love!

And to the Amplify Publishing team, particularly Brandon Coward. Without the talented and dedicated work of a publisher, this book would not make its way into your (the reader's) hands.

I'd also like to thank the hundreds of leaders I've had the privilege to coach over the years for entrusting me with your journeys and for the invaluable lessons I've gleaned from each of you. Working with you has been akin to reading a captivating, beautiful book—I always find myself eagerly wondering, "What happens next?" Your stories and experiences have enriched my own path immeasurably.

A multitude of individuals have served as my teachers, guides, and sources of inspiration over the years and deserve my heartfelt appreciation. To my yoga teachers across the decades, from Mark Stevens—my first teacher at Sun and Moon Yoga in Arlington, Virginia, who told me, "Just breathe"—to Doug Keller, who trained me as a yoga teacher and thoroughly explained yoga's true integration. I recall my disbelief (disagreement) when I first heard Doug say, "Yoga isn't about the poses. The poses just help you prepare for meditation." Although he teaches and reaches across the globe, I will always consider him "my" yoga teacher. And thanks to the many teachers in between, including Susan Van Nuys, Pat Pao, Mary Beth Markus, and so many others.

I extend my deep gratitude to all my coach teachers over the years, particularly Chris Wahl, Alexander Caillet, Mike McGinley, Frank Ball, Dave Snapp, the late great Neil Stroul, and my Great-28 cohort colleagues at Georgetown University. Looking back, I am humbled by how resistant I was to leaving the safe shores of my "known," yet each of you patiently guided me toward embracing the art of coaching rather than simply teaching or mentoring. Your dedication and encouragement have profoundly influenced my journey. Thank you for believing in me and helping me grow in this transformative profession. And to my MCC mentor coaches, Jennifer Starr and Ellen Fulton, for helping me take the leap toward mastery.

What would my journey have been like without my friends who supported and challenged me throughout the years? A special thank-you to my talented and longtime friend Janet Ply, as we shared stories on our paths to publication.

Finally, I want to recognize the individuals whose lives intersected with mine during periods of what might be termed "successful exhaustion" rather than being mindfully successful. I apologize for any unintended discord I may have caused. I hope that these encounters served as fertile ground for growth and introspection for you, as they did for me.

Thank you all.

The years teach much that the days will never know.
—Unknown

ABOUT THE AUTHOR

Margo Boster is an executive and leadership coach and yoga teacher with more than twenty-five years of rich experience in diverse senior leadership roles in information technology across private sector companies and governmental organizations. She has spent the last fifteen years as an executive and leadership coach, supporting leaders, including CEOs, US military generals, and other senior executives, to reach their peak potential.

Margo holds the prestigious Master Certified Coach (MCC) credential from the International Coaching Federation (ICF). She further contributes to the coaching community as an ICF Mentor Coach and Assessor, supporting other coaches in enhancing their coaching skills. She is also an adjunct faculty member in Georgetown University's Coaching Program, a facilitator and mentor coach at Flatter Leadership Academy, and a guest lecturer in Arizona State University's graduate program for Environmental Leadership and Communication.

Drawing on extensive studies of psychology, anatomy, philosophy, neuropsychology, and adult development, Margo has crafted a coaching philosophy that integrates the latest insights from these fields with her decades of leadership experience. Her approach is enriched by over three hundred hours of training as a certified yoga teacher, blending the wisdom of the mind-body connection with modern leadership principles.